Testimonials

"As an expert in the dating industry I have read many different books on building healthy relationships. I highly recommend *Cupid's Playbook* as it not only offers a step-by-step guide to finding love, it helps you avoid the pitfalls that can keep you from achieving that love connection."

Julie Paiva *Founder and CEO, Table for Six Total Adventures*

"As a matchmaker, I loved reading *Cupid's Playbook*. The Kaisers have written an easy step-by-step guide to finding love. *Cupid's Playbook* gives singles clear direction while preventing the dating fumbles that keep singles from finding a passionate, yet healthy love relationship."

Patti Lafond *Professional Matchmaker, Meet me for Lunch, Anchorage, Alaska*

"I highly recommend *Cupid's Playbook* as a worthwhile read for single love-seekers of any age. Our dating culture is more complex than ever and Jeannine and Keith have addressed each of the critical issues that are facing men and women who are dating in today's wild world."

Julie Ferman *Personal Matchmaker and Dating Coach, www.CupidsCoach.com*

"*Cupid's Playbook* has totally equipped me for the game of love (and I'm not talking bows and arrows). The Kaiser's tools and techniques have given me a clear game plan to find the love of my life."

Frances Rostick *Author of Miss Match: A Seriously Funny Look at Dating*

"*Cupid's Playbook* is definitively a must for every single's bookshelf. It's a very complete insight into the dating process, applicable to any age group or life stage. Fun, personal, and full of practical solutions..."

Fernanda & Adela Ayensa *Matchmakers, Dafer, México (Mexico City)*

"*Cupid's Playbook* is a humorously written, yet insightful tell-all book about dating. The exercises in this book are designed to help singles get out of their own way and find the love they desire."

Heidi Bilonick *Relationship Expert, President, CEO, Coach Heidi and Company*

"Who needs Cupid when you have inspirational, down to earth, real in your corner love coaches like Jeannine and Keith, who walk their talk. If you aren't lucky enough to take Jeannine and Keith's seminars in person, this book is the next best thing."

Susan Bradley *RN, Love Coach, & Author of award-winning* **How to be Irresistible to the Opposite Sex** *and* **How to Flirt without Appearing Like you are in Heat!** *www.LovingUniversity.com*

"I just finished reading *Cupid's Playbook* and it's been a long time since I've read such a concise, informative and all-encompassing self help book about dating and finding love. Not only that, but Jeannine and Keith's personal experiences really help show the reader that they know what they are talking about. I have several clients that I will be giving it to as a gift! *Cupid's Playbook* is a must read for any single person looking to start dating again or wondering what has been going wrong in their dating world. The hands-on exercises really make you think and help you figure out what you need to work on before starting on your plan to meet your next relationship."

Sheryl Williams *Ignite Matchmaking Service, Denver, Colorado*

CUPID'S PLAYBOOK

How to Play the Dating Game to Win!

by
Jeannine and Keith Kaiser

EMERALD
BOOK CO.

Published by Emerald Book Company
Austin, TX
www.emeraldbookcompany.com

Illustrations and cover art by Tim Bower.

Distributed by Emerald Book Company
For ordering information or special discounts for bulk purchases, please contact
Emerald Book Company at PO Box 91869, Austin, TX, 512.891.6100.

Publisher's Cataloging-In-Publication Data (Prepared by The Donohue Group, Inc.)

Kaiser, Jeannine.
   Cupid's playbook : how to play the dating game to win! / by Jeannine and
Keith Kaiser.

      p. ; cm.

   ISBN: 978-1-934572-36-8

1. Dating (Social customs) 2. Man-woman relationships. I. Kaiser, Keith. II. Title.

HQ801 .K35 2010
646.77   2009938275

Printed in the United States of America on acid-free paper

09 10 11 12 13 14   10 9 8 7 6 5 4 3 2 1

Contents

Acknowledgements

We want to express our gratitude to Barbara Magoon for challenging Jeannine to date 100 men in a year. Her goofy request has changed Jeannine's life forever by launching her into a career that she loves and helped her find Keith, the love of her life.

To our children, Jessica, Derrick and Ashley: Thanks for eating takeout and frozen dinners so that we could finish this book. We owe you many home-cooked meals. You have been wonderfully supportive in our seminars and in our lives and we appreciate it more than you can possibly know.

To our good friend Dory Willer: We want to thank you for being a guiding light in Jeannine's life and throughout her career. Thank you for getting Jeannine into the coaching profession and for being Keith's personal coach early in our relationship. You have ultimately enriched our lives and helped to change our life's direction.

We want to express our appreciation to our parents, brothers, sisters, and extended family for helping to shape who we are and bearing with us as we share our personal experiences about growing up in an effort to help others to find their ideal mate.

We want to thank Emily Johnson for her work editing the first draft of our book. We truly appreciate all your help and seeing our book through the reader's eyes, as well as for all your support at our seminars.

Tyler Theurer is our irreplaceable knight in shining armor. We can always count on him to help out at our seminars even if it means dropping whatever he is doing and flying up from Los Angeles. Thank you Tyler!

Jan Gilman has always tirelessly volunteered her time to do whatever is needed to make things run smoothly. Thanks for being our rock and consistent support.

Theron Chow is our brilliant business advisor. His guidance has helped us move to the next step in expanding our seminar series.

We are grateful to our editor Deborah Burstyn for all her guidance, hard work and for making our book shine by using her eye for detail and her clever insights.

Our deepest gratitude to Lindsey Hart, our personal guardian angel. She rescued us many times. Her eye for detail, efficient speed and extensive knowledge of graphic design and book formatting helped us create a wonderful final product.

We want to extend a big thank you to Georgia Greenlee who helped develop the vision for a great finished book cover.

To our friends in the media who have helped us to become well-known as dating coaches throughout Northern California: We are grateful for your faith in us. Thank you for providing us with the inspiration to do more for both the singles community and couples seeking greater intimacy and passion.

- We want to express our gratitude to Baltzar Ibaez and Maria Todd from Movin 99.7 radio in the San Francisco Bay Area for having Jeannine as the love doctor, on their show as a regular guest.

- Thank you to Susan Safipour of *Diablo Magazine* for writing a great article about Jeannine. This helped significantly in making the work we do more prominent.

- Thank you to Stephanie Simon for attending Jeannine's flirting class and writing such a fun article on your experience.

- Thank you to our friend Robin Fahr of Channel 30 who has hosted Jeannine on her show, *Conversations with Robin Fahr*, numerous times and has been a wonderful supporter.

- Our gratitude to Henry Tenenbaum of KRON TV for interviewing Jeannine on his show and getting the word out in the community about our work with the singles community and with couples.

And last, but certainly not least, to all of our clients: Thank you for allowing us to guide you on your soul mate quest. You are our inspiration for writing this book and the work we do.

Introduction

Congratulations! When you bought this book, you took your first significant step towards finding your ideal relationship. There seems to be a zillion books out there on dating and relationships. They have some great information in them, but they are in bits and pieces. To be successful in dating and relationships, you would have to read an over-whelming number of these books and put those puzzle pieces of information together to create a plan of action on your own.

We wanted to write a different book. One that would help you create a comprehensive plan to find the person of your dreams while giving you information that would guide you in creating a healthy, loving and lasting relationship.

You might be entering the dating world after a divorce or the death of a beloved partner. Maybe you have never been married or in a long term committed relationship. It could be that you've never had a serious love relationship or you've had a string of unsuccessful relationship disasters. It doesn't matter. This book will help you through the dating process and towards a successful relationship or strengthen your current relationship.

At the age of 36, Jeannine got divorced from a man she now

humorously refers to as her "practice husband." When she re-entered the dating world, she had no idea how to meet single people. She had been out of the dating scene for 13 years. Back then she had met most of her dates through school or work. But now Jeannine wasn't in school and she wasn't working. Her big question was, "Where are all the good single people?" What she didn't realize at the time was that she was trying to start in the middle of the dating process.

Going out to find single people is not where you need to start. You need to start with taking a good hard look at yourself and determining your readiness for a relationship. Unfortunately, this step is missed by many people already in relationships and is usually a significant factor in the failure of the relationship. You need to know why you desire a love relationship. Are you trying to fill a void in your life? Do you feel incomplete without a love partner? Do you even know what you want?

If you don't clearly know what you need or want in an ideal mate, it will be hard, if not impossible, to find that person. They might be right under your nose and you won't see them. This book will help you answer these questions and get you going on your "soul mate quest."

You wouldn't go out to find a fulfilling career by going door-to-door hoping that by chance that you will find that ideal position. You have to give some thought to what you want to do. You might need to get some additional education or training. You have to write a resume that will grab someone's attention. Additionally, you have to know what questions to ask and prepare to answer questions on an interview. Dating is a lot like finding a fulfilling career; you have to take the time to prepare yourself for the process.

We are going to walk you through the entire process, step by step. It wouldn't matter if we put you in a room now with 500 good potential partners because if you don't understand the process you are going to leave the room feeling alone and defeated. You must know what you want, how to mingle and how to ask good questions. Also, it would not matter how many good single people you meet if you don't feel deserving of a partner who treats you well, adores you and honors you. You will just be spinning your wheels and/or attracting every loser in the room who is looking for someone to be their personal doormat or feed their ego through your attention.

We wish we could be your guardian angels, wave a magic wand and instantly find the love of your life for you. Unfortunately, it doesn't work that way. You have to do some work and some soul searching. You have to be honest with yourself. You cannot change what you don't acknowledge. If you truly do the work outlined in this book, you will be in a great position to find your ideal mate and create a lasting, loving relationship.

Once you have laid the foundation, we will guide you on your journey to find quality single people and show you how to land a date. We will let you know how to mingle with the opposite sex at single events. We will share with you some of our favorite and most revealing questions to ask on your dates. Our creative list of dating venues will have you excited to plan your next date!

But we won't stop there! You will learn to step beyond finding a date to building towards a quality relationship that will rock your world for a lifetime. We will help you understand how you can create a wonderful relationship where you will get your needs met while feeling loved and adored. And your partner will feel the same way!

How you do anything in life is how you do everything. How you read and interact with this book will determine your level of success and is a direct reflection of how you live your life.

There will be those people who read this book and don't do a single exercise we've outlined. These are the people who do as little as possible just to get by in life and find they are struggling in many aspects of their life. They wonder why they are unsuccessful in love!

Will you be a person who reads this book and does some of the exercises? Will you look at the exercises and conclude that you don't really have to do "that exercise" because you already know the answer? In the area of love, are you doing just enough to look like you are out there looking for your ideal mate? Sometimes you are putting in a lot of effort, but at other times, you are just checked out. You will reach success by not only knowing what to do, but feeling it is the right thing to do and doing until it becomes habit. That takes commitment and practice. Please do the work!

You might be a person who opens this book and approaches it with great skepticism; questioning almost every line we've written. Could it be that you look at love and question if there is truly someone who can be your soul mate? Do you know what a soul mate is? Do you look at other people's motivation and wonder what the person wants from you?

We are going to challenge you to be the person who picks up this book and goes at it with an "all out attitude." Even if you do not play full out in life for the sake of finding your ideal mate, do it NOW! Have an open heart and mind and be willing to do all the exercises in this book. Put 110% of yourself into the process.

Be sure to checkout our website for even more information and special offers at www.SMQMastery.com. You can also sign up for our free newsletter to keep you up to date on all the latest dating and relationship news.

So, if you are ready to roll up your sleeves and get a little dirty, let's get started with creating your passionate love relationship!

CHAPTER 1

Dating IQ

We began writing this book because many of our clients told us that we were a wealth of information about dating and relationships. We've learned much of what we know not only from our research but from our clients and our own life experiences. We hope that by sharing some of these bits of wisdom, you will be closer to finding your own ideal relationship. But the number one motivation for writing this book is to show that if an individual works to secure a strong foundation first and then builds upon that foundation with their partner, they will have a healthy, loving and lasting relationship.

We learn much of what we know about dating and relationships through the school of hard knocks. Most of us have a Masters Degree in what doesn't work. The opposite of this doesn't necessarily translate into what does work. That is where we come in. This book will walk you through your own personal experiences to extrapolate the learning from your successes and failures. It is not a one-size-fits-all concept. Each person will walk away with their own newfound knowledge and game plan for approaching dating and relationships. This book will help you create a strong foundation for being successful in today's world and will lead you to find your ideal mate and create a loving and passionate relationship.

Your Dating IQ is a culmination of your experiences in dating and your observations of the key love relationships in your life. We filter the data through our mind like a computer and out comes the beliefs we carry with us about finding love. Sometimes, those beliefs actually hurt you in the dating process and in relationships. So we have to make changes to our beliefs by examining new ways of looking at our negative life and dating experiences. This book will give you a fresh perspective on the process of finding a truly healthy love relationship and help raise your Dating IQ.

Guiding singles on their quest for the ideal relationship is our greatest passion. You get the benefit of all our research, knowledge and experience in this book. Our clientele consists of men and women of all ages who are seeking their ideal mate. With their permission, we have included what we have learned with them in this book as well.

Have you ever wondered why there aren't any classes taught in high school about relationships, dating, marriage and child rearing? Guess it might be tough finding someone qualified to teach these courses because most people are just trying to figure it out. It might be a case of the blind leading the blind.

What would it be like to be given information that would help you to avoid painful lessons about love that most us learn from the school of hard knocks? With the divorce rate in the United State approaching the sixty percent mark, we think it is time that we looked at how we make decisions about relationships and how we interact once in a relationship. This book is about just that, making healthy decisions.

Never in history have there been so many singles re-entering the dating world in mid-life. For centuries, people got married and, for the most part, stayed together until "death do they part." We aren't saying that they were happy, but the fact is they stayed together.

More often than not, men would look for a woman who was sturdy and who they thought would be a good mother to their children.

Marrying for love was not as important as having a person who could help run the household. Having a partner to raise a family was a necessity because running a household was hard work. The man was out on the farm planting crops, running cattle, repairing fences and doing all the other men's work. The woman was washing clothes on a scrub board after hauling the water in from the local stream, milling the wheat to make the flour to make the bread, churning-the-butter to put on the bread, and sewing the family's clothes all with a baby on her hip. Things have changed!

We no longer make decisions to get married out of necessity. Both men and women now have the option to stay single. A woman can work in corporate America, make a substantial living, have children without being married and not have to wear a scarlet letter on her dress for a lifetime. A man can stay single and take his clothes to the cleaners, pick up a quick meal at a local restaurant, fast food joint or the prepared section of the grocery store, and hire a housekeeper to clean the house. Although we have some amazing luxuries, we believe that this really has complicated the world of dating and finding love. There is a whole new set of rules and expectations out there and people seem to be struggling to figure them out.

You have a choice on selecting a mate and how to make this selection. But are you attracting and selecting your mate to feed your ego and not your soul? Do you want that person who looks good to the outside world, the trophy girlfriend or boyfriend? Do you want someone who will make you feel good for those few moments when you are having sex? Are you putting your emphasis on their bank account or career before you look at them as a person? Today's dating world is a grand new adventure. With so many people looking for love in mid-life, we must forge a new road towards success in an unexplored arena. We view this unique time in history as an opportunity to lay a foundation to help singles develop healthy, off-the-charts, love relationships, something that has eluded many of us throughout our lives.

Make no mistake! The media has influenced how we look at love relationships. Movies, pop songs and television have made us believe that finding love is filled with high drama and exciting unexpected meetings that lead to marriage. That makes for good entertainment but it just isn't real and adds nothing to raising your Dating IQ or finding your ideal mate.

Are you a real sucker for those chick flicks like *Sleepless in Seattle*, *The Wedding Planner*, and *Pretty Woman* and all the rest? These may be fun movies to watch but life often doesn't give us the fairytale ending they have led us to expect. These movies put the emphasis strictly on the chemistry between two people. The movie stops there. Chemistry plays a part in seeking your ideal mate but compatibility is the glue that makes any great relationship work.

We are all imprinted with the fairytale stories of Cinderella, Snow White, Sleeping Beauty and the other princesses in fantasyland. (Most girls today may only watch the Disney movies.) These fairytales condition a young girl to believe that the person of their dreams will come along, sweep her off her feet and make her life complete and wonderful. A few dances on the ballroom floor and a shoe that fits just right are the only things you need to be swept away to the fairytale ending. These are not realistic stories. Love does not happen this way.

Men have also been misled by television and movies. Watching movie heroes like James Bond, Indiana Jones, John Wayne, and of course Clint Eastwood in his bad boy roles, to name but a few, have left men with the impression that they need to be mysterious, lead an adventurous life, defend a woman using heroic measures and then leave her breathless and desiring more after making passionate love to her. Then and only then, can he get the most desirable woman! Now, add to the mix that that the modern woman wants a man who can communicate on an intimate level and we have created the unobtainable, not to mention the outright ridiculous!

Recently, there have been many reality shows about people seeking the perfect soul mate, life mate, husband or wife. Although these shows offer a humorous evening of television viewing, we cringe at how flippant they are about relationships. With limited information, gathered in a fantasy environment, the participants are making the decision to choose a life partner. It might make for good television ratings, but sends a very disturbing message about how to select a mate for life and/or treat them in a relationship. It is disturbing that there are so many men and women so desperate to find their ideal mate that they would subject themselves to a reality television situation where they can't be themselves because they will be sent home empty-handed, broken-hearted and disgraced on national television.

We have coached thousands of people on dating and relationships. We cannot believe how many people are walking around thinking that love is going to strike them like a lightning bolt, and just like that, they will know they have found the right person. Who makes up this stuff? We are talking about chemistry when we are referring to lightning bolts. Chemistry is not love, it is lust. We are all for chemistry, but chemistry without compatibility is a recipe for disaster. You have to know what you want first. You can be hit by a zillion lightning bolts and miss the right person because you don't know what you want or you aren't ready for the right relationship.

If we had a dollar for every time someone said, "You can't help who you fall in love with," we could pay off the national debt. (Okay, that is a fantasy). You can't entirely control the chemistry, but you can have a level head and make a good decision about taking the relationship forward. Just because you have good chemistry does not make the person the right match for you.

With all this misinformation coming at you in rapid succession, it is important to raise your Dating IQ to avoid falling prey to the media hogwash you are being fed. Let's get real about dating, relationships and falling in love and make our own dreams come true.

Jeannine's Story

I have had my own quest for finding the right relationship. My first marriage ended in divorce in 1994. Determined not to make the same mistakes again, I had to identify those mistakes. After blaming my ex-husband for many years for the break-up of our relationship, I finally got real about my contribution to the failed relationship. I had chosen the wrong relationship. Yes, I said that I chose the wrong relationship.

At twenty-one years old, I began dating my "practice husband." Like most young adults, I believed that I was very mature. "The Queen of Dating" was a title I could have easily bestowed upon myself. I had dated a few dozen men by the time I was twenty-one and had several long-term relationships lasting six months or longer. There were several men who were just lovers, which I mistakenly labeled as relationships. After all, we were having sex, so we must be in a relationship. Silly me! So, being the mature person that I thought I was, I was ready to get married. Nothing could have been further from the truth. At twenty-one years old I had no idea who I was or what the heck I needed or wanted.

My parents divorced during my senior year of high school. Although my parents' marriage was rocky for as long as I can remember, it was a level of security that I could count on. My father was a very good provider. My mother is a wonderful, loving person. When I was growing up, she was an involved caretaker.

I lived in a beautiful custom-built house with a swimming pool in an upscale suburb of San Francisco. My siblings and I attended private schools up until high school. It was the dream life that many only hoped for. But behind closed doors, it was really a different story.

We lived in a house that was often full of tension and fighting between my parents. There were lots of good times and laughter too, but the tension never seemed far away. My father was quite strict. My mother tried to compensate by being more lenient. However, the one area where they presented a united front was in giving the outside world the impression that we were this perfect little family. That is what people did in our town back then, pretend everything was perfect even when it wasn't. People were shocked when our family fell apart on March 18, 1977. That was the day my mother went to an attorney and filed for divorce. My normally stoic father left the house visibly shaken. I will never forget that day as long as I live.

People who marry young are more likely to get divorced. My parents were one of these divorce statistics. My mom and dad got married when they were in their early twenties and really didn't know each other very well. They worked very hard to keep their marriage together. They were Catholic and divorce was not to be taken lightly. Although I have many fond memories of my childhood, I can't remember my parents ever being really happy together or being in love and devoted to each other.

When my parents divorced, the secure life we had known came to an abrupt end. My father had provided everything financially for our family. Suddenly, we all needed to pull together to make sure the bills were met and we had food on our table. My father gave my mother money, but it didn't even come close to what we needed. I turned over my pay from my job as a waitress at a local ice cream parlor to my mother. My sister and brother did the same. I graduated from high school not knowing what I was going to do. There wasn't any money for college. What was I going to do with my life?

Three years after my parents' divorce, I began dating my "practice husband." I felt insecure, alone, incomplete and unhappy. I felt that by finding a solid relationship, I would feel complete and happy. Just like that line from the movie, Jerry McGuire, "You complete me," I was looking for someone to complete me. This is such hogwash. No one can complete you! They can complement you, but never complete you. I wasn't marrying the man. I was marrying to feel more complete and alleviate my own personal fears. I married his ability to provide a good income. I also married him for his stable family.

After eleven years of marriage that included bringing three wonderful children into this world, I filed for divorce. The last thing I wanted to do was go out into the dating world again. I wasn't looking forward to dating, but I did want to find a wonderful passionate love relationship. I rolled up my sleeves and began to navigate the dating world. I didn't realize that I needed a compass, a map and some idea of where I was going.

It wasn't long before I was in another relationship. I fell in love hard and fast. He seemed like the perfect match for me. I had known this man since my early twenties. Our life experiences seem to run parallel, we had similar value systems, we had this amazing spiritual connection, and the sex was off the charts. He loved my children and I loved his children. So what went wrong?

I have never completely understood the demise of this relationship. I justified that the timing was off. Neither of us had completely severed our relationships with our former spouses and there was lots of drama in both of our lives. But the truth being told, he treated me poorly. Not all the time, but enough that I should have seen red flags flying in my face. I let the chemistry override his actions. He emotionally hurt me time and time again and I repeatedly let him back into my life. It is obvious to me now that I did not believe that I was deserving of being treated wonderfully all the time. However, when this relationship ended, it broke my heart.

Again, I was in a hurry to get into another relationship. So, I went on the hunt for the next boyfriend. I dated like a wild storm. One day, I was having lunch with my best friend. Barbara, who was married to her ideal mate. She boldly pointed out that I was always in a relationship or was dating to get into a relationship. I had never been single for more than a few minutes. She then asked me a mind-blowing question. "Jeannine, who are you outside of a relationship?" I had no idea. I had been someone's girlfriend or wife ever since I started dating at age sixteen. This realization was the beginning of my transformation.

When I have revelations like this, it is in my nature to do something about it. Once, a friend of mine told me that she could order food for me at any restaurant because I was so predictable. We were sitting in a restaurant at the time and getting ready to order. "She'll have a Cobb Salad with blue cheese dressing on the side and an iced tea," she confidently told our waitress. It was exactly what I was going to order. She was right. I was predictable. For the next year, I committed to being unpredictable by going to different restaurants and ordering new and different cuisines. I learned that there were many foods I liked that I had never even tried. I tried sushi, Thai food, Indian food and other ethnic delights and really enjoyed them. When I realized that I was also predictable about getting into relationships too quickly, I was committed to changing that, too!

Barbara challenged me to date for a year without getting into a relationship. But she went one step further and challenged me to set a goal of dating one hundred men in one year. I took the challenge without even thinking that this would be a problem. After all, it is less than two dates per week.

You might be thinking, "How did she meet all these men?" It wasn't as hard as you think. I told all my friends about my new goal. Knowing my history, they all wanted to be supportive. So they set me up with a number of men. I also met men on the internet, through personal ads, in singles groups, church groups, and in the grocery store. I had more blind dates with men in that one year than I ever had in my entire life. I had an absolute blast. With nothing to lose, I became really ballsy.

My dates became a playground for asking bold questions. Sometimes I may have ticked a man off, but I learned something. This marathon year of dating enabled me to evolve a list of qualities I desired in my ideal mate. As a result, I learned a lot about men in general and ended up with a comprehensive list of what I wanted in my ideal mate. Four months after completing my list, I met my husband Keith.

I raised my own personal Dating IQ by embracing who I am as an individual, learning from my past, getting clear about what I wanted and then took action to find my ideal mate. The result is an amazing relationship with my husband. We have been happily married since Valentine's Day 2000. Keith complements my life beautifully. The process I created to find my husband was actually fun and hugely successful. Together, Keith and I are going to share the process with you. So buckle your seat belt. You are in for a fun and exciting ride. Let's raise your Dating IQ.

Keith's Story

Like my wife, Jeannine, I was also a child of divorced parents. I was thirteen years old and just getting ready to go into high school when my mom and dad divorced. At the time, and through most of my early adult life, I didn't think my parents' divorce had much impact upon my life and relationships.

It was not until I examined my own life in a little more detail and especially some of my own failed relationships that I realized how much impact it had. Until I did, I did not benefit from the learning that came from that experience or those of my own failed relationships. When I finally I took the time to explore my own journey through life, I was able to start making decisions based upon introspection and understanding of past experiences, and not out of habit and reaction.

After my parents' divorce I became that rebellious teenager that parents fear. My normally mild mannered behavior escalated into being the bad boy; cutting school, getting into fights, frequent sexual relationships, street racing my hot-rod cars and motorcycles and other activities not generally considered appropriate at any age. For the most part, I managed to keep these activities from my parents and my school. I guess I thought I was pretty smart.

I couldn't wait to get out on my own. I graduated from high school a year early. I think they were glad to get rid of me. I had always worked after school and even managed a gas station during my last year of high school. I was going to be promoted to district manager but because I was not 18 yet I could not get a bond. However, after graduation I got a well-paying job requiring membership in the Teamsters' Union, which only fed my bad boy reputation even more, not to mention my wallet. Within days after my eighteenth birthday I married my high school girlfriend. Although we were great friends, we started our married life together really knowing nothing about each other and it turned out our goals were diametrically opposed. Both of us had married each other to get away from home, but neither of us liked where we ended up. After a year or so we called an end to the relationship. Often, two people's insecurities come together to form the perfect reason to get married, but not form the perfect union.

I left my high-paying job and took a position for a fraction of the pay in computer programming. My father advised me to start a career and go to college. I was wise enough to take his advise. I met a woman at work and fell in love. Now, you would think that because I had just left a marriage, I would choose to just date and have fun being single. But instead, I became involved with a woman who was getting divorced and pregnant.

We got married and I instantly became a stepfather. Again I started a serious relationship (marriage) with neither one of us knowing much about each other or parenting. Although our goals were similar this time we were both strong willed and competitive and the combination was toxic. I often contemplated leaving the relationship, but I didn't want another failed marriage. After all, I was only in my mid-twenties.

About ten years into our marriage, I was driving home from a long day at work and had a near fatal car accident. My sports car hurtled at high speed down a steep embankment, end over end. I arrived at the hospital barely clinging to life. You might think I should have been considered this one of the worst things to ever happen to me, but this accident was my wake-up call. When you stare the Angel of Death in the face and live to tell about it, it has the potential to change you as a person. Therefore, I decided to change a lot of things in my life. Putting an end to this very stormy marriage made the top of my list.

Over the next decade or more, I did what I should have done in my early twenties; I dated. I blew through dozens of relationships, had some one night stands, and even explored being "friends with benefits." This whirlwind of dating helped me to discover who I was as a person and as a man. It also helped me discover who I was not.

It was during this time, that I began to do some serious introspection and self-evaluation. Now I had finished college, and had my MBA as well as a very successful career in the Defense Industry. I had been a program manager, operations manager, division manager, CFO, COO and sat on the board of directors for both profit and non-profit companies. But I began to have an awakening. I finally realized I wasn't nearly as smart as I thought I was. I imagine it being similar to being an alcoholic, only my substance of abuse was my career and how others saw me. I needed to get with the 12 step program and became a "recovering smart guy" or recovering smart ass as most of my friends and associates would say. To this day I am still recovering and fighting a relapse of the need to know everything and be able to fix anything!

It was also at this time I began writing my relationship list and reading anything and everything available on the subject. The further I got into writing my list, the clearer it became that I was not in the right relationship because I was not the right person. I spent a lot of time focusing on me and my relationship skills. I examined my past with an eye toward learning from my mistakes and my misconceptions. It took some time and a fair amount of effort but things started to become much clearer that I needed to be with a very different type of woman than I had chosen in the past.

Not long after this I met my wife, Jeannine. She was unexpected, refreshing, challenging and wonderful all at the same time. We began as friends, having a glass of wine or a cup of coffee after her class at the University of San Francisco and chatting on the phone. This went on for months as I realized that my feelings for her were growing stronger. When I reviewed my relationship list, I realized that I had found the woman I was looking for.

Many people were skeptical about our relationship, pointing out that Jeannine was not my type. She certainly was not the type of woman I had dated (mostly out of habit) in the past. In reality, she was my type. All the other women I had dated were just the prelude to my discovery of what I needed and wanted in a loving and healthy relationship.

It wasn't always smooth sailing. I had to endure Jeannine finishing her college degree, court battles with her "practice husband," and I had to get to know her three children and work to bond with them as a happy loving family. Throughout all of the good times and the turmoil, I saw how well we worked as a couple and as a family. I knew that if we could work through the difficult situations, and grow closer in the process, we were meant for each other. Jeannine and I dated for almost two years before I popped the question on Valentine's Day 1999.

We were married the following year on Valentine's Day 2000 with the blessing of three great children and have all lived happily ever after. Okay, the happily ever after part is the fairytale we have been telling you to avoid. Relationships take work and although we are extremely happy together, as a couple, and as a family, we continue to work at it ... but the work is fun. Jeannine has challenged me to be the best that I can be. Together, we have discovered what it takes to create a deep, intimate, loving relationship and family.

I hope that our journey will help you on your quest to find your ideal mate. You don't have to come from the perfect family background. We certainly didn't. You can have a rocky dating history. I did! You might have a couple of "practice marriages" under your belt and your partner might too. It doesn't matter! In fact, Jeannine and I are going to show you how you can use all of this life experience to find your ideal mate.

Falling In Love With You!

You have probably seen those women and men who can attract the opposite sex like bears to honey. You look at them and think, "I am just as good looking. How come people aren't flocking to me?" There might be a reason that could very easily be fixed. Would you like to learn the secret to having people be magnetized to you? Then read on soul mate searcher!

We have a friend named Julie. Julie is cute, but there are many women who are much more beautiful. Yet when you put Julie in a room of people, she soon has an entire group around her laughing and having a great time. Julie has something special. She really likes herself as a person and it shines through. She is confident in who she is. Even being a bit overweight does not dampen her confidence. Even back in high school and college, Julie could attract any man. Other girls admired her but were a bit jealous. People might say that Julie knew how to play the dating game better than anyone else. But, Julie isn't playing a game. She is just comfortable with herself.

The difference between Julie and most women-and men too-is that Julie has some great internal dialogue. She felt good about herself and her internal dialogue reflects that. The result is an even higher level of self-esteem.

If your internal dialogue is negative, it can be really tough on your self-esteem. Let's take a minute to look at your own personal dialogue. What is your internal dialogue telling you? Are you constantly telling yourself that you are too fat, too thin, not cute enough, not a stylish dresser, not funny enough, too shy, too loud, etc? You can easily convince yourself that you don't measure up. If you are going to be really dateable, you are going to have to examine your internal dialogue and possibly make some changes. By doing so, you will raise your game to a whole new level, not only in the dating world, but in life.

One of the biggest steps in becoming a successful dater is to accept YOU. If you can't accept something about yourself then make the decision to change it. But really, you don't have to change a thing about yourself. It doesn't matter. If you love yourself, no matter what, then you are very dateable.

So, what is internal dialogue? It is simply the things we say to our self. It is that little voice in our head telling us that we measure up or we don't. No, you aren't schizophrenic. What most of us are doing is paying attention to what we like to call, the Itty Bitty Shitty Committee or IBSC. This is our own inner dialogue in which we are highly critical of ourselves. Your inner dialogue might sound like this:

I don't like my nose.
I am too fat.
I am too thin.
If there is loser in the room, they will find me.
People don't find me attractive.
I laugh too loud.
I'm too short.
I'm not smart enough.
I don't earn enough money.
I don't have an interesting career.

I have too much baggage.
I feel like a fraud most of the time.
If people really knew me, they wouldn't like me.
I don't have enough hair.
My hair is too thin.
My hair is too thick.
I have no sense of style.
The people who say they love me, leave me.
I am not lovable.
I don't have anything interesting to say.

The more we say something to ourselves, the more we believe it to be true. We actually look for supporting evidence that these things are true. Would you say these hurtful things to a friend or loved one? Of course you wouldn't. Then why do you say them to yourself?

EXERCISE: Discovering Your Internal Dialogue

(Are you going to do this exercise? Remember, you will get more out of this book if you do the exercises!

Keep a pad of paper with you for a week. Pay attention to your internal dialogue. If you say something negative, hurtful or unproductive to yourself or about yourself, jot it down. Make yourself aware of your inner dialogue. At the end of the week, find a picture of yourself from when you were about three or four years old. While holding that picture, read out loud your negative self-dialogue.

You are still the same beautiful human being you were as a young child. You are the same person. How does it feel to tell that young child that they:

- *Don't measure up?*
- *Aren't pretty or handsome enough?*
- *Aren't smart enough?*
- *Just aren't enough?*

We all have imperfections. Imperfections make us interesting. If you are striving to be perfect, it will never happen. There are no perfect people, just people pretending to be perfect. Personally, we are bored and uncomfortable around people who pretend to be perfect. They do not share any funny stories about how they screwed something up or moving stories of triumph over adversity. If someone is pretending to be perfect, we get these flashes of feeling judged on our perceived imperfections from these seemingly perfect people. You cannot really connect with someone who pretends to be perfect because they are not being real. So do you want to be one of those people or someone people easily can connect with?

It is human nature to gravitate to someone who likes themselves and is happy with their life. We are not talking about the people who going around bragging and tooting their own horn to anyone who will listen. That is simply an arrogant person who is really an insecure jackass. We are referring to someone who is comfortable in their own skin. They have quiet inner confidence that can be felt. How did they arrive at that place in their life? They have control over their inner dialog. Their inner dialogue is primarily positive. It is not that negative dialogue doesn't creep in every once and a while, but they become aware and shift back to positive dialogue.

You have to learn to deal with your inner dialogue. Before you can get really comfortable in your own skin, you have to learn to handle the *IBSC*. We are going to give you the secret to doing this by first identifying what you are saying to yourself.

There may be things that you need to address. Maybe you have some self destructive behavior that is keeping you from moving forward with your life. Are some of your behaviors hurting other people? These are not flaws. These are problems that need to be resolved. If your behaviors are hurting you or others, get professional help to deal with these behaviors. You will be happy you did.

You have two choices with an imperfection: learn to accept the imperfection or decide to change it. Either choice is fine as long as you can accept yourself. Accepting and loving yourself is the key to finding a fulfilling love relationship.

Sometimes you just can't get past the imperfection. We had a client who was a sharp successful executive with a witty personality. She was in her mid-thirties and she hadn't had a date in two years. She didn't like her appearance. She felt that she had let herself go over the past few years. When we met her in person, her hair wasn't styled and she wasn't wearing makeup. She was wearing an outfit that hid her nice figure because it was oversized and outdated. She wanted a makeover but she didn't know where to go to get a new look.

We assembled our makeover team. We cut, colored and highlighted her hair, giving her a modern, but easy to style haircut. She wanted natural looking makeup. We gave her a new look by enhancing her beautiful eyes, and keeping her lips natural, but still adding radiant color. Lastly, we got rid of all the clothes in her closet that were out dated and hid her great figure. We added a few new outfits that made her look and feel beautiful.

Within a week, she had three dates. It wasn't because of the make-over. It was because she felt beautiful. She actually carried herself differently and interacted with people more confidently. She wasn't afraid to be seen or noticed.

Sometimes, making small changes will help you feel better about yourself. You need to decide. Our client was the same person, but she felt different and her inner dialogue changed. Her new dialogue was, "I feel beautiful." That small shift made the difference in helping her on the path to finding find her ideal mate. She is now in a wonderful relationship.

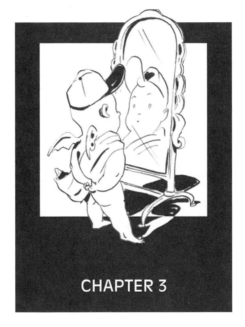

CHAPTER 3

Would You Date YOU?

The key ingredient in the magic formula for becoming successful in love and dating is self-love. Self-love is the key to finding true love. It gives you the ability to fully love and embrace someone else and to accept that someone can love you.

One of the exercises we give our clients is to make a list of all the things they would change about themselves. For most of our clients, they can make this list in just a few minutes. Then, we turn the table and ask them to make a list of all their positive qualities. Most of our clients struggle with this list.

Spending time on our positive attributes is not a common occurrence. How often do you look at yourself in the mirror and compliment yourself? Most of us are critical of what we see looking back at us. When it comes to our positive inner attributes, we pay even less attention to these.

Let's look at you and find the qualities about you that make you a good catch. If for even a second the thought ran through your head that you aren't a good catch, pay close attention to this section of the book. (Your IBSC is working overtime.) Everyone has wonderful qualities that make them special and unique. It is important that you identify yours.

We are not cookie cutter versions of each other. Thank goodness! The fact that we are uniquely different makes the world an interesting place to live. We all have qualities that make us special.

We want you to spend some time writing down the things that make you special and unique. We are going to help you get started in the process. If something on our list resounds with you, add it to your own list. This is where we encourage you to plagiarize!

- I am a good listener.
- I am funny.
- I have a good sense of humor.
- I have a nice smile.
- I am kind.
- I am honest.
- I am considerate.
- I can support myself.
- I am good at decorating.
- I am artistic.
- I am musical.
- I am a good dancer.
- I have wonderful friendships.
- I have a good relationship with my family.
- I am creative.
- I am successful in my career.
- I am talented in my profession.
- I am genuine.
- I am faithful.
- I have a strong belief in a higher power.
- I am spiritual.
- I manage money well.
- I love to explore new places.
- I am daring.
- I like a variety of different foods.

- I am comfortable in a group.
- I am comfortable talking one-on-one.
- I like myself.
- I am healthy.
- I am a good cook.
- I am a good host/hostess.
- I am good at facilitating change.
- I empower others.
- I am a good mother/father.
- I am good at persuading people.
- I am good at managing things.
- I am good at planning events.
- I bring joy to others.
- I am good at creating trust.
- I am good at picking out clothes for myself and others.
- I am intuitive.
- I am good at seeing possibilities.
- I am good at pursing possibilities.
- I am a happy person.
- I am good at figuring out how things work.
- I have a green thumb.
- I have good time management skills.
- I am good at building things.
- I am organized.
- I am good at researching /investigating things.
- I am in good shape.
- I am resilient.
- I am passionate.
- I am outspoken.
- I am an observer.
- I read people well.

- I am athletic.
- I have a good singing voice.
- I am a good friend.
- I am a good lover.
- I am a good writer.
- I am good at solving problems.
- I am good at fixing things.
- I love performing.
- I am good at building relationships.
- I am someone people can count on.

This list is just a starting point. If something on the list doesn't resound with you, it means you have different gifts and talents. This list is simply a tool to help jog your mind into action to create your own list. Some of you were going down the list and thinking, "I'm not good at this or that." So what! You are good at many things and those are the things that make YOU unique and special. Those are the things you need to embrace. Remember, you have to "be the one" to "find the one."

EXERCISE: Why You Are a Great Catch List

Make your list of good qualities and put them down on paper. Take some time to notice what you like about your body. Look at all the tiny little things that make up the whole you. Look at your eyelashes, the shape of your eyes, the freckles on your nose, the shape of your fingers and toes. Take a peek at your fingernails and toenails. How about your eye color or the shape of your ears? Do you like the shape of your face? Do you have long legs? Do you have nice looking hands? What parts of your body can you just take some time to love and appreciate?

Take the time to examine your roles as a friend, sister, brother, aunt, employee/employer and any other role you play in life. Look at your talents and interests. They make you unique and special.

Shifting your view about yourself is a major turning point in finding a love relationship. If you don't value yourself for who you are, how can you expect someone else to do that? How can you love someone else for who they are if you can't even do that for yourself? Do you see why this is so important? Read your list every day to remind you how awesome you are.

Mirror, Mirror on the Wall

Jeannine speaks about her challenge with body image:

One of the loudest voices of the IBSC is the one shouting about body image. I personally have struggled with body image for most of my life. I remember when I was in fifth grade and had to get a physical before I started school in the fall. During the physical, the doctor told my mother that I was overweight and should start a weight loss program immediately. This was surprising news to me. It never crossed my mind that I was overweight, because I wasn't. I was just going through puberty. I had a slight thickening around the waist that many women get before we start our first menstrual period. In the next six months following the physical, I shot up four inches and thinned out. But because of that doctor, it was now imbedded in my mind that I was over-weight.

In my early forties, I had a real struggle with weight. I have always been a small person. I might have been ten pounds overweight at times, but usually, I was a size 7 or less. When I took hormones to get pregnant, I gained weight rapidly I went from a trim size 7 to a size 20 in six months. It seemed like I would go to sleep and wake up bigger. So, I know what it is like to be overweight. Being a larger woman did not make me a different person, but people did make some hurtful comments. Some members of my family were quite brutal. There was nothing I could do about my weight until the hormones leveled out again. I continued to eat healthy and exercise, but I did that for me, not to lose weight. I realized that my weight did not make me a better or worse person. I liked myself and that was that. But it wasn't easy maintaining my self-esteem in a highly critical society.

We are not going to pretend that there isn't a level of prejudice in our society, especially when it comes to issues of physical appearance including weight. One of the greatest concerns expressed by our female clients is their belief that they will never get married because they are overweight. We hear the same complaint from men just not as often. If you are very overweight, you may indeed be limiting your options in the dating world. Can you do anything about it? Are you paying attention to what you are eating? Are you exercising? Have you investigated any health issues that might be contributing to your excess weight? If you aren't addressing these issues, what is stopping you? If you are choosing a Snicker's candy bar and Haagen-Dazs over dating and sex, you may need to make different choices. Which do you want more?

Your weight doesn't make you loveable. How you feel about yourself does. You can fall in love and get married even if you are 20 pounds or 100 pounds, or more, overweight. Our question is: Are you settling for less than you deserve because of your weight? If so, you need to change your weight or change how you view yourself.

Attitude is 90% of getting past anything that is limiting you. If you believe that something about you is keeping you from having what you want, then it will! If you believe something to be true, it is our nature as humans to find supporting evidence about that belief.

We were working with a woman who believed that she was unattractive to men because she was 20 pounds overweight. It had been more than a year since she had been out with a man. Now, we had met this woman in person and she had the most beautiful chestnut color hair, skin to die for and a gorgeous face. She was curvy and very sexy. Not only that, she was a lovely, interesting person. So we knew that the reason she wasn't getting dates had nothing to do with her appearance or personality. It was her IBSC!

She had been married before to a man who was a body builder. Her husband was very body conscious. He was hard on himself and very hard on her. Not only did he verbally criticize her, he rejected her sexually if she gained a few pounds. Through this very destructive relationship, she drew the conclusion that she was only lovable if her body was perfect.

She wasn't getting dates because she believed that she wasn't datable or lovable until her body was in perfect condition. In order to protect herself from getting shot down in the dating world, she had built an emotional wall around herself that made the Great Wall of China look like a picket fence. She was cold and distant when she was in the presence of single men. As a result, men weren't going to approach her for fear of being shot down.

We worked together to bring the wall down, brick by brick. It really didn't take too long. We took a sledge hammer to the wall by examining her inner dialogue and making some serious changes to how she talked to herself.

Another exercise we did with this client was to encourage her to go on thirty dates in thirty days. Those dates were with her, not a man. Everything she did was geared towards making her feel beautiful and sensual. She got facials, massages, took a bubble bath and did other things that made her feel pampered. These dates helped her begin to appreciate herself. Within a month of completing these exercises, she began getting asked out because she was looking at herself differently.

It could be that someone told you that your nose is too big or your ears stick out or you're too short. Someone can say something to us once, but we say it to our self hundreds or thousands of times until it becomes bigger than life. Many times it isn't even true. It was just someone's shallow opinion. You can be as beautiful as a Miss Universe contestant or as handsome as a soap opera star and still dislike things about your body. You just need to embrace your uniqueness.

When you learn to honor yourself and take care of YOU, you can begin to invite a life partner into your life that will do the same. Your partner will honor themselves and honor you in the process.

Your attitude about you will determine your level of success in dating and the rest of your life. This is totally within your control. Learning to love and honor yourself is a key element for attracting your ideal mate. The greater your self-love, the faster you will find that wonderful partner you are seeking.

CHAPTER 4

Who Wrote the Rules to The Game of Love?

When you were a child, did you ever make up a game? You might have combined a couple of games like tag and dodge ball. Let's imagine you were actually playing tag, but you were tagging your opponents by hitting them with a ball. There were no written rules, like in football, baseball and other sports. There were just the rules you create as the game progressed. As you played more, you might have added more rules to make it easier or more difficult. For instance, you might have added a rule like: You can only hit someone in the torso, otherwise it doesn't count. Well, the *Game of Love* is a lot like making up your own game. There are no written rules to the *Game of Love*. They are simply the rules each person makes up in their head. These rules are called beliefs.

The problem with the *Game of Love* is that often people come into a love relationship with different sets of beliefs or rules. We each have our beliefs about love and love relationships. Each time you begin a relationship with someone, it is as if you are playing a game and she/he doesn't know your rules or beliefs. They are playing their own game. However, people who are playing the *Game of Love* believe that everyone is playing by the same rules-theirs!

So, how do we get these beliefs or rules? The beliefs we have about love relationships are derived from viewing relationships around us. The most significant relationship is the one that existed between your parents. What you experienced in your home can be very different from the experience of someone else. Maybe your parents were divorced when you were very young or you were part of a blended family due to remarriage. What if you or your potential partner came from a home where there was domestic violence? Your views about love and marriage can be dramatically impacted by the environment in which you were raised. Most families have dysfunction. Some families are just more dysfunctional than others.

Let us demonstrate this by presenting a bizarre scenario meant to simply make you aware that what we learn through our experiences within our family is not always shared by others.

Let's say that you grew up in a family that celebrated a good meal by throwing their wine glass into the fireplace. When you went to your aunt and uncle's home for dinner, they did the same thing. Everyone in your circle of friends and family did this at the end of the meal. So you learned to accept this as normal behavior.

Then a boyfriend invites you to dinner at his parents' home. At the end of the meal, you throw your wine glass into the fireplace in celebration of the wonderful meal. Everyone around the table gasps in horror. You just threw the Waterford crystal into the fireplace and it broke into hundreds of pieces. You conclude that you shouldn't throw expensive stemware into the fireplace.

The next time you are invited to someone's home for dinner, you estimate the value of the stemware and conclude it isn't expensive, so you throw it into the fireplace. Again, you get the same gasp and people looking at you like you are crazy.

You begin to realize that it isn't the price of the stemware that is the cause of their reaction; the behavior of throwing the glass into the fireplace is the problem.

We develop beliefs about the world around us from our experiences in the world. Beliefs are not truths or laws of the universe because they are not the same for everyone. Simply put, a belief is something we think is true based on our experiences.

We once worked with a young woman who came from a family who was very stingy about saying "I love you." Her parents rarely uttered these words as a form of affection and love. They never said "I love you" to their children! They would often tell the children that they were proud of them often, but did not say I love you.

This woman was in a relationship with a man and the relationship was in trouble. She cared deeply for this man, but was unaccustomed to saying "I love you." On the other hand, he came from a family who were "I love you" junkies. His family would throw these three little words around casually. When this man told her that he loved her, which was frequently, she did not respond in kind.

His frustration grew as he waited for her to utter those three little words. He talked to her about it. He pleaded with her. Still she did not tell him what he needed to hear. Finally, he gave her an ultimatum: "You have to tell me that you love me within the next month or I am going to leave." Ultimatums do not work, especially in matters of the heart.

Because of this woman's upbringing, saying "I love you" was a monumental commitment. She believed that saying "I love you" meant that she was ready to marry him and she wasn't sure she was ready to marry him. She was unable to muster up the courage to tell him the tremendous weight the words carried for her. It isn't surprising to learn that this couple broke up.

This is a clear example of two people coming into a relationship with two different rules in the *Game of Love*. Could this relationship have been salvaged and flourished? Yes! But it would have taken patience and understanding on the man's part to understand that her family's culture was very different than his. The woman would have to understand that she had a limiting belief about saying the words "I love you" and she would have needed to establish and embrace a new belief.

This young woman had formed a limiting belief. A limiting belief keeps you from moving forward in life and love.

Jeannine's Relationship Imprints

Sometimes, we can grow up in the same family with others and wonder how we view life so differently. I grew up in a conventional family with six children. We were all really close in age. We shared the same home, the same parents, many of the same friends, the same religious upbringing, the same schools and same advantages in life.

At family functions when my siblings and I start talking about our childhood, I often wonder, "Did we really grow up together?" I remember things so differently. Sometimes I don't remember something at all but everyone remembers me being there. There are times when I will tell a story and my family looks at me like I am missing a screw. They don't remember that happening! Here are people who experienced the same thing but registered different emotional imprints.

Emotional imprints have an impact on how we choose a love relationship. As we grow up, most of us witness the relationship between our parents. We arrive at beliefs about marriage and relationships based on what we witness in our home.

When I was a young child, the only experience I had to gauge family "norms" was my exposure to my own family. There were glimpses into other families when I went to friends' homes to play or visited my uncle and aunt's home for the holidays. But what I knew about family "norms" was based on my own experiences in my own home. I believed that every family was like my family. My limited experience about marriage came from watching my parents.

We had a traditional home with traditional roles. My father was the breadwinner and my mother the homemaker. My mother, along with my sisters and me were responsible for all of the household chores including cleaning, grocery shopping, childcare, school involvement, and the majority of the cooking. (Dad made breakfast on Sunday mornings.)

When my father came home from work, he expected dinner to be ready to go on the table. He expected the house to be in good order, after all that was my mother's job. Dad did most of the yard work with the help of my two brothers. They mowed the lawn, cleaned the pool, weeded the yard and made repairs to the home and cars. In addition, dad was responsible for paying the bills and doing the taxes.

In my mind, I believed that my father wasn't very happy with how my mom did her job. Just before he came home, there was the hustle and bustle of six children scrambling to put away our school books, toys and turning off the television. (We weren't supposed to watch it during the week but mom let us anyway.) The table had to be set and dinner ready to be served when dad walked through the door.

I don't know if it was my mother's fear of getting my dad upset that drove this chaos, or if my dad really had become upset when the house was in disarray and Mom was trying to avoid a conflict. I do remember heated arguments between my parents including raised voices. Mostly they seemed to argue about housework, raising the children and money.

When my mom went shopping for groceries or clothing, you could cut the tension with a knife. My dad had a strict budget which he expected my mom to adhere to. He had six children to feed, provide clothes for and educate. When mom overspent, he would get upset and my mom would vehemently justify her expenses.

I remember birthdays and Christmases fondly in our home. There didn't seem to be any fighting about the money spent on gifts for these occasions. My dad made a big deal out of my mother's birthday, often taking us to a nice restaurant where Mom ordered lobster complete with one of those lobster bibs. Dad would buy her a cake that was served at the restaurant. Also, he always bought her something special on Christmas and we all waited with great anticipation for the unveiling of his gift.

We had lots of good times as a family, especially on vacations. There was lots of laughter and poking fun at each other. The siblings got along well despite the typical squabbles. But the relationship between my parents never seemed to be a close partnership. It rarely felt warm and loving. Through my young eyes I drew the following conclusion about marriage:

- *Parents argue with raised voices. When things calm down, they act like nothing ever happened.*

- *The one who makes the money makes the rules.*

- *The man has the last say on any big financial decision.*

- *In a marriage, you shower your partner with attention on holiday birthdays and anniversaries and just co-exist the rest of the time.*

- *The man of the house is the disciplinarian.*

- *The wife does the housework and cooking. The husband makes the money, takes care of the yard and cars.*

- *The mom takes care of all the children's needs and activities.*

- *If you aren't earning any money you need to ask permission to buy something for yourself or spend money on the children.*

If you ask my parents if these were messages that they wanted to send me, they would shout NO! They would even be appalled at the beliefs

I took away from my upbringing. However, to me the messages were loud and clear.

Here is how some of these filters impacted my "practice marriage": In my "practice marriage" my husband believed that the man had the right to make major decisions without my input. This caused some of our biggest arguments. I remember when we were buying a new car and we had narrowed the scope down to two. It was a Saturday and I was pregnant with our second child. So I stayed home when my husband went to purchase one of the two cars we had selected. I was happy with both of the choices and joyfully waited for him to return. Three hours later he pulled up in the driveway with a Jeep that was not one of the two choices. This was the car I would be driving for the next decade. I had no say in the decision. I was really upset but it also felt normal at the same time.

I spent most of my marriage fighting not to be controlled and not giving up my voice. But I unknowingly chose a relationship that was controlling and where I had to battle to prove that I could not be manipulated.

I was fighting to find my voice in the world. I wanted to ask for what I wanted, needed and deserved in life without being punished. My belief was that I would be punished for expressing what I desired. Punishment took the form of withholding affection and personal interaction. Any time I asked for something, I braced myself for a fight or worse.

My life experiences told me that I could only get what I wanted with conflict. I didn't understand that you could have a logical, calm conversation with someone and get your needs met. The only form of relationship interaction I knew was conflict and I was comfortable with that. I wasn't comfortable with asking for something in a logical calm way.

Another source of great conflict and frustration in my first marriage was the discipline of the children. My "practice husband" wasn't a disciplinarian. He would ignore the children's behavior and wait for me do say or do something. I was really frustrated because I believed that he should be taking the lead when it came to discipline. My "practice husband's" father was passive about discipline and left the discipline to his mother. My mother did not discipline. She would say the words "wait until your father gets home," and I knew I was in for it. Our contradictory belief about who should take the lead on discipline left us without any discipline in the house. What a mess!

One of the silliest behaviors I developed was shopping and hiding my purchases. Even though I made as much money as my husband, I didn't feel I had the right to go out and spend money without asking for his permission. I would buy clothes at the end of a season and not wear them until the next year. When my husband would ask if it was new, I would honestly say that it had been in my closet for a long time. My husband didn't give me any reason to think he would get mad. However, because of what I witnessed in my parent's marriage, I was trying to avoid the pain that might occur from my shopping sprees. It was a very dishonest way of behaving.

I duplicated my parent's marriage in another area. I married a man who was really sweet on Christmas, Valentine's Day, anniversaries and my birthday. He was more than generous with gifts and attention on those days. But on a day-to-day basis, I felt I didn't matter. I had a full time job outside the home. When I came home from work I cooked, cleaned and took care of the kids while my husband sat on the couch and watched television. No matter how much I begged, cajoled, or screamed he wouldn't budge. I grew to resent him.

When my "practice husband" and I fought, we fought intensely. We planted our heels into the ground and there was no compromise. Neither of us desired compromise. We were both looking to win. We didn't fight fair. When I look back at my first marriage, I see that *although I believed that I was creating a marriage unlike my parents, it really was the same. With each argument, my "practice-husband" and I walked away with more emotional scars. After years of these fights, we had so many resentments that, like my parents, divorce was imminent.*

So why am I sharing my experiences and life filters with you? We all create beliefs about love and relationships based on our life experiences. You have your own life experiences and life filters. Those filters contribute to your success or failure in your key love relationships. What do you believe to be true from your life experiences? What might you be doing to sabotage your relationships?

In order to effectively look at the possibilities of your limiting beliefs, you must look at different aspects of a love relationship.

What beliefs have you taken away from watching and experiencing your parents' relationship? If you don't want your relationships to be like your parents' relationship, then what do you want instead? Take the time to do this next exercise. It will bring you great clarity.

EXERCISE: Discovering Relationship Beliefs

Answer the following questions based on what you observed from watching your parents' or other significant committed relationship (grandparents, aunt & uncle, foster parents etc.).

How do people in love show love for each other?

How does a married couple handle money and investments?

How does a married couple spend time together?

How do they spend time apart?

Do they have friendships outside of the couple relationship?

How are the chores and household responsibilities divided?

Who is the spiritual leader in the family?

How are big decisions made between the couple?

Who is the disciplinarian of the children?

How do people in love disagree/argue?

How do they handle problems?

How do they interact on a day-to-day basis?

How do they show respect for each other?

What type of activities do they do as a couple?

By becoming aware of your own personal beliefs about how a couple interacts, you can examine how you have taken these beliefs into your own love relationships. Sometimes they have served you well. Other times, you might be over compensating for how your parents' interacted as a couple. You might have had a mother who was quiet and accommodating. You become outspoken and demanding because you don't want to be like your mother. We refer to this as a "wide swing." You don't know what is in between so you go to the extreme opposite.

You also might be retroactively trying to "fix" your parents' relationship by recreating their relationship and then attempting to act differently. Let's say that your father was an excellent money manager. You didn't like that your father left your mother out of making decisions about money, so you marry someone who isn't good with money with the intent of creating a relationship where you work together to manage the money. You want your partner to learn how to manage money and work with you to help pay bills. However, your partner isn't good at it so you are constantly disappointed. Trying to fix your parents' problem can create new problems in your relationship.

Sometimes we recreate our parents' relationship because it is what we know and are comfortable with. We call this "going home." This is why so many people who come from abusive homes become abused or abusers. Even though they don't like the environment they grew up in, it is all they know. Most people don't attempt to gain new coping skills before going into another relationship. "Going home" is often the reason many people get married to someone just like mom or dear old dad.

How we believe the world operates is an accumulation of all the beliefs we have formed throughout our life. Some of our beliefs are positive and help us form healthy relationships, positive work and life ethics, and help us forge a path for personal growth. However, some beliefs limit us in one or all of these areas. We simply call them "limiting beliefs."

How do you form a limiting belief? It is a bit complicated, but we will explain the process.

1. You observe or experience something in life. Example: You come home from school and you learn that your father has moved out and your parents are getting a divorce. There was no warning. You didn't see it coming.

2. You experience emotions such as fear, sadness, powerlessness, confusion or anger.

3. You begin to formulate thoughts or questions in an attempt to understand what you are experiencing emotionally. You might ask, "Doesn't Dad love us any more?" "Why didn't he tell me he was leaving?" "Shouldn't I have known something was wrong?" "Dad couldn't have really loved us or he wouldn't have left."

4. You then form a belief:

- People who love me leave me.
- I can't tell when something is wrong because I am not very observant.
- Men can't be trusted. They say they love you and then they leave.

5. Once you believe something to be true, you will find evidence to support your new belief. If a friend's parents divorce and her father moves out, you see more supporting evidence. You might find supporting evidence while watching a movie or television show that portrays a man leaving his family. You might pick up one of the tabloid magazines and read about some celebrity who leaves his/her partner suddenly. Last week this same couple was so in love and now it is over.

Because you believe that love is so fragile, you might become very cautious and unsure in a love relationship. You might need a lot of reassurance from your partner that they love you. Your limiting belief about love and marriage can keep you from having a healthy fulfilling relationship.

Let's take some time to examine a few possibilities of your limiting beliefs. Once you identify them, you can change them. Again, this list will simply be a tool to jog your mind into action and identify your personal limiting beliefs.

- I have to fight to get what I want in a relationship.
- I have to be perfect to be loveable.
- I have to give up a part of myself to be in a relationship.
- I have to give up my personal power/freedom to get married.
- Relationships are full of conflict.

- There are no healthy relationships.

- People I love leave me.

- The person who makes the money makes the rules.

- If I am a stay at home mother/father, I have to prove my value by doing housework, cooking and errands.

- There is too much competition out there.

- Men want to date younger women.

- Women want to date men with money.

- I'll never meet the right person.

- All the good men/women are taken.

- It will be too hard to get married because I'm over forty.

- I have to settle for less than I desire if I want to get married.

Watch how we shift these limiting beliefs. We just take a new view of each. You can do the same for your personal limiting beliefs.

Here are some examples on how to shift your limiting beliefs. These may seem simplistic. They are! Shifting your limiting belief to an empowering belief is just claiming something different or looking at it from a new perspective. Have some fun seeing how simple it can be!

These are just a few examples of some limiting beliefs about relationships. Some might be true for you or it could be that none are true for you. By looking at your past relationships and the relationship you observed between your parents, you can extract your own personal beliefs. The next step is to determine if that belief is limiting you in creating your ideal relationship. If so, create a new belief.

Shifting Your Limiting Beliefs about Dating and Relationships

In the past, I believed I have to fight for what I get in a relationship.
Now, I believe that I can ask for what I want and be given what I desire by a loving partner.

In the past, I believed that I had to be perfect to be loveable.
Now, I believe that someone will love me just as I am.

In the past, I believed that I have to give up a part of myself to be in a relationship.
Now, I believe that my partner will be supportive of me being my authentic self.

In the past, I believed that I had to give up my personal power/freedom if I got married.
Now, I believe that marriage will give me more personal power and freedom because my spouse will be very supportive of me.

In the past, I believed that relationships are filled with conflict.
Now, I believe that conflict in a relationship is an opportunity for growth and forging new paths and boundaries.

In the past, I believed that there are no healthy relationships.
Now, I believe that learning to communicate can bring me a happy healthy relationship.

In the past, I believed that people I love will leave me.
Now, I believe that I am worth fighting for in a love relationship.

In the past, I believed that the person who makes the money makes the rules.
Now, I believe that I can be an equal partner in a marriage including financially, even if I am not working outside the home.

In the past, I believed that if I am a stay at home mother/father I have to prove my value through housework.
Now, I believe that I don't have to prove my value. My spouse will see my value as a person and my partner will cherish my contribution to the family.

In the past, I believed that there is too much competition out there.
Now, I believe there are new single people entering the dating world every day.

In the past, I believed that men want to date younger women.
Now, I believe that many men are looking for an energetic and mature well- balanced woman.

In the past, I believed that women only want to date men with money.
Now I believe women are looking for an overall good man who will make them feel loved and cherished and that is ME!

In the past, I believed that I'll never meet "the one."
Now, I believe if other people are meeting terrific partners then so can I.

In the past, I believed that all the good men/women are taken.
Now, I believe I am a good catch and I'm available, so there must be other singles out that are a good catch, too!

In the past, I believed that if I don't have sex with him/her, he will lose interest in me.
Now, I believe the right man/woman will be willing to wait until I am comfortable having sex with him/her because he/she values me.

In the past, I believed I was in a relationship if we were having sex.
Now, I believe that I don't have to have sex to move from dating into having a relationship. Being in a relationship is determined by the

level of emotional intimacy created between my partner and me.

In the past, I believed there is something wrong with me because I haven't been married yet and I'm forty.
Now, I believe I haven't settled because I deserve to be in the right relationship and others admire me for my resolve.

In the past I believed that I have to settle for less than I desire if I want to get married.
Now, I believe that the right man/woman is out there looking for me.

These are just beliefs and they are only true if you believe that they are true. You now know how to shift a belief to a more empowering belief.

There are a few common limiting beliefs about dating that can set you up for failure, disappointment and a broken heart. The five most common limiting beliefs have come up time and time again when we have coached singles. We are going to call them love myths. So let's just throw these myths on the table and take a look at them so we can finally put them to rest.

Love Myth 1: Love can conquer all

Have you ever been in a relationship with a partner who had some serious shortcomings or emotional problems? You thought that if you just loved them enough, you could help heal their wounds or make them a better person.

You can't heal someone. You can't change someone by loving them. The truth of the matter is you are setting yourself up for heartache and disappointment. You will drain your energy, beat your head against the wall and work your fingers to the bone expecting to see the results you desire. You are wasting precious time and energy that could be spent finding a person that meets your needs and desires right now.

Love Myth 2: Love at first sight

The belief that you will know true love the minute you meet "your one and only" is a belief that many of us secretly hold. We have been conditioned to think that this is how love works through the avalanche of books and movies we soak in where a couple finds that instant connection. It feels so good watching those movies or reading these books because we hold on to the hope that it could happen to us, too.

This isn't love at first sight. It is lust or infatuation at first sight. It is the physical chemistry or intrigue between two people. Love takes time to develop. It is well beyond the sexual attraction two people experience. Love consists of a deep respect, honoring and acceptance of each other despite our imperfections and shortcomings. It is that lasting affection like the twinkle in your partner's eye when you walk into the room even after fifty years of being together. It is being that elderly couple who still holds hand while taking a stroll.

Love Myth 3: Your true love will meet all your needs

You should not expect someone to meet all of your emotional and physical needs. You should not be expected to meet all of their needs. A healthy relationship is an interdependent relationship where you mutually rely on each other but you are able to take care of yourself. If you expect someone to meet all of your needs and desires, you will spend your whole life alone or feeling short-changed in a love relationship.

Expecting someone to anticipate your every need is also a big part of this myth. You and your partner need to be able to express your needs to each other, while not expecting your partner to fix everything. It is unrealistic and exhausting to put yourself or to be put in a situation where you are trying to read your partner's mind and anticipate their needs. You set yourself up for failure and disappointment.

Love Myth 4: There is only one true love in the world for you

If this were true, someone whose relationship ended in divorce or death of their partner would be destined to live the rest of their life unfulfilled by another love.

The truth is that there are many potentially great partners out there for each person. We can't tell you how many partners are out there for you, but we know there are many more than you can imagine. If you set your sights on finding "the one," you might miss out on a fabulous relationship.

Think about this! If there is only one true love for you, you have a one in a six billion chance of finding that one special person. Heaven forbid that they live in another country. The reality is that there are hundreds if not thousands of great potential partners for you.

Great relationships are not found, they are created. You will learn more about this later in the book.

Love Myth 5: Powerful sexual attraction or chemistry must be love

Both of us (Jeannine and Keith) have been guilty of believing this myth several times in our lives. We hung on to relationships that didn't have much to offer outside of the bedroom. Confusing powerful sexual chemistry with being in love can draw you into an unhealthy relationship, blind to its incompatibility.

You can justify feelings that don't really exist in order to keep having sex with a person. In our society, it is not okay to engage in a sexual relationship just for the pleasure of having sex, so we often manifest in our minds feelings of love in order to continue the sexual relationship without guilt.

Can you identify with any of the common love myths? Have you been involved in a relationship that presented one or more of these love myths? If the answer is yes, then you have now identified one of your vulnerabilities when selecting a love relationship.

We all have limiting beliefs about dating and relationships. If you can identify your limiting beliefs, you can change them. Take some time to look at yours. But first, you have to be honest with yourself. By identifying your own limiting beliefs, you can become much more successful in the dating process.

These examples are simply shifts in your thought process. If you change where you place your energy and attention, you will change your relationships. You have to decide to leave your old beliefs behind and embrace your new empowering beliefs. You can reinforce your new beliefs by finding supporting evidence in the world and relationships around you. If someone else can have it, so can you. If you want something different, then claim it, believe it, and live it with self-confidence. It really is that simple.

EXERCISE: Identify Your Limiting Beliefs

Take the time, right now, to identify you own limiting beliefs about dating and relationships. Find a new empowering belief that serves you and your goals to have a healthy life and love relationship.

Write down your new beliefs. These will be your new mantras. Keep them in a place that you can review these new beliefs daily. The more you say them, the quicker you will accept them as your new beliefs.

By doing this exercise, you will become clear about the beliefs you have extracted from your upbringing. You will then have the choice to accept these beliefs as your personal truth, or determine if you want something different instead.

Maybe you know what don't you want. That's okay. That is something you can explore in the dating process. Dating can give you insight into other ways of being in a loving relationship.

CHAPTER 5

Cupid's Relationship Map and Game Plan

Your dating or relationship history can be a window into understanding your dating patterns and behaviors. You might have dated many men/women or maybe just a few. Either way, you have established a pattern of behavior in dating and relationships.

The first time we have a successful date that leads us to being in a "relationship," we are excited. Subconsciously, we store away our method for getting into that love relationship because, of course, it worked. Our tendency is to repeat the pattern hoping for the same result: LOVE! It is kind of like the directions on a shampoo bottle: rinse, lather, repeat. We feel we have uncovered the secret to getting into a relationship.

But what happens if it doesn't always work? Most often, what we have discovered was an isolated incident of success. We have now created a limiting belief: If I want to get into a relationship I need to do A, B, & C and I will get into a relationship. When we believe something to be true, even if it isn't true or doesn't work for everyone every time or in every situation we can get stuck in a rut because it seemed to work once or twice before.

The primary reason Jeannine dated 100 men in a year, was to

attempt to break her pattern of behavior that existed for her from the day that she began dating. That every man she dated had the potential to be her next relationship. It didn't matter if they were a match for her or not. Jeannine's limiting belief was: "I am no one without someone to love me." This might sound insane, but this was true for her at the time.

This is why it is important to look at your dating and relationship history. Do you have a dating history that is sabotaging your future for the ideal relationship? It is not something that is easily identified. In the moment, it might not seem significant. But if we take a bird's eye view of our life and relationships, we might be able to shine some light on our life and love choices.

The first step is to map out all the positive and negative qualities in your past partners. Also this includes the positive and negative qualities in your mother and father that you have observed over the years. The next step is to identify any patterns that may be repeating in your dating and relationships. The following two exercises will help you examine the qualities of your past relationships and those you have observed, and provide a window into your relationship patterns.

EXERCISE: Mapping Your Desired Relationship Qualities

Take a piece of paper and list all of the positive and negative qualities of both your mother and father and all the men or women you have dated List the negative and positive qualities side-by-side on the paper. When you finish, look for patterns. Do these people have similar qualities? Do you date one type of person and then date someone who is quite the opposite? Are your selecting mates that are just like dear old mom or dad? Are you improving in your selection process? Or is it getting worse?

	Positive Qualities	Negative Qualities
Mother/Step Mother		
Father/Step Father		
Past Relationship		
Past Relationship		
Past Relationship		

EXERCISE: Mapping Your Relationship Patterns

Take a look at all the dates/relationships you have been involved in during your lifetime. Let's define a love dating/relationship. For this exercise, if you dated someone for more than two months, then evaluate the relationship. If you dated someone less than two months but had sex during that time, evaluate the relationship. You might have a few and you might have a few dozen. All of them are significant in determining your patterns in dating/relationships.

Answer these Questions	*Name*

Where did you meet?

Who initiated the first date?

How long did you date?

When did you first have sex?

Why did you have sex?

Did your behavior or expectations change after having sex?

What signs indicated the relationship was faltering?

What did you do when the relationship started to falter?

Who ended the relationship? Why?

By examining the qualities of your past relationships, you have a window into your relationship patterns.

Where did you meet?

If you see a pattern of meeting people in the same way or same place and it isn't working out, it is time to change things. One of our clients met most of her boyfriends at Alcoholic Anonymous meetings. She was a recovering alcoholic. Although she had done a lot on self-work, the men she chose had not.

Another client would only date women he met through friends. He started the relationship on a friendly basis and then pursued the romance. It is wonderful to have a friendship with your life partner but he was setting up this pattern because he was using friendship as his only conduit to romance. He had set himself up for a pattern of failure. None of the choices he made were the right relationships for him. But they were easy because he was in his comfort zone. He had to step out of his comfort zone to become successful. Once he did, he got into a wonderful relationship.

Is there a pattern of where you are meeting your dates? Do all or most of your dates come from an internet dating site? Are you meeting at clubs or bars? What is your pattern?

Who initiated the first date?

If you are a woman and are initiating the first date, you probably are not successful at dating. A man has to feel as if he has won a prize. You can flirt with him, smile and have eye contact. It is even okay to tell him that he seems like a great guy. It is okay to put yourself in situations to be noticed by a man but let him ask you out!

If you are a man who is not initiating the first date, you are being cowardly or lazy. If you are waiting for the woman to ask you out, you might be waiting a long time. Or worse, you probably are settling for less than you deserve. Maybe you are shy. Maybe you lack self confidence. But if you want to make improvements, you are going to have to step it up if you are going to get the women—or anything else in life for that matter.

How long did you date?

Is there a pattern in your dating history? Do you date someone a few months and then lose interest? Do you stay in a relationship for a long time even though you know there isn't a great match? Do you have lots of first dates but not many second dates?

One man we worked with had many first dates and very few second dates. We discovered that he was discussing all his imperfections on the first date and asking women if they were willing to take an HIV test before having sex. He didn't understand that these two factors were killing his chances of getting into a relationship. We all have imperfections but you don't lead with those on a first date. Secondly, asking for an HIV test is like going to a job interview and asking for a promotion before you even get the job.

Another female client had an entire list of deal breakers. If a date displayed any of these on a first date, she was done. If they were late, even by a few minutes, she would not date them again. If they answered their cell phone on the date, she wouldn't date them again. She eliminated men for the slightest infraction.

When did you first have sex?

More and more couples are having sex early in the relationship. Do you have sex within the first few dates? How does that impact the development of the relationship? Are you in a committed, monogamous relationship before having sex? Are you assuming that you are in a committed, monogamous relationship because you are having sex. Is there a pattern?

At a singles event, we met a man who had a reputation for sleeping with many, many women. Often he would date and have sex with several women. He told us that women are irresponsible when it comes to asking for an exclusive sexual relationship. Women just assume that he is only having sex with them. He explained that women get upset when they find out he is dating and having sex with other women, but he never committed an exclusive relationship of any sort.

Although we think this man's approach to dating and sex is questionable, we have to admit he is right. You can't just assume that you (male or female) are in a monogamous relationship without a discussion. You have to request it.

Why did you have sex?

We have sex for a variety of reasons. It feels good to be touched and feel connected to another human being. Do you have sex because you feel you might lose the potential relationship if you don't? Do you have a few too many drinks and find your inhibitions lowered and BOOM you are in bed? What are your patterns?

One client of ours got into her first serious relationship after having sex on the first date. Believing that sex meant that she was in a relationship, this client had sex on most of her first dates. She even pressured men into having sex. When the men never called again, she became angry and very frustrated. She felt they were deceiving her. She was actually deceiving herself into believing that this is how one gets into a relationship.

Did your behavior or expectations change after having sex?

A beautiful, smart woman admitted to us that her behavior changed drastically once she started having sex with a man. She wondered where the relationship was going and started putting more demands on the man. Her insecurities drove the man out of the relationship and had him running for the hills.

Another male client wasn't sure if he should call the next day to assure his date that he was still interested. He didn't want her to think he wanted a serious relationship partner, but he didn't want her to feel that he wasn't interested in her either.

In both of these situations, sex complicated the relationship. Do you change your behavior after having sex and how?

What signs indicated the relationship was faltering?

There are usually signs when a relationship is going downhill. One or both of the parties begin to withdraw. There are more spats often about seemingly meaningless things. The phone calls and time spent together become less and less frequent.

Sometimes, when the "honeymoon" ends, a couple is unable to negotiate a realistic and healthy relationship. Their differences and expectations are vastly different.

What happened in your past relationships? What signs did you see? Is there a pattern?

What did you do when the relationship started to falter?

Your reaction to the "signs" that the relationship is faltering can either bring the relationship back on track or speed up its demise.

Having honest discussions about how you feel can be a healthy way of getting the relationship back on track or making the decision to end the relationship on a good note.

One of our male clients desperately wanted to be in relationship that led to marriage. If he felt the relationship faltering, he would throw every bit of romance he could at the relationship. He would send flowers, leave little notes on her car, or plan a romantic get-away. Everything but what he needed to do, talk with his partner. He was constantly heart-broken because he tried to show her love and she rejected him.

Who ended the relationship? Why?

If you find that you are always ending the relationships, ask yourself

WHY? Is there a pattern? Or are you always the one getting dumped? Do you hear the same thing from your partners when the relationship ends?

One of our friends ended every one of his relationships and had many regrets about his decisions. He was so afraid to be rejected that he found reasons (many of them very silly) to end the relationships before he got hurt. He left in his wake many broken hearts and confused women.

Another woman was dumped so often that she described herself as "a piece of garbage that was left on the curb." Most of her relationships ended because she was too clingy and needy. The message was clear but, she just kept ignoring it. She was doomed to repeat the pattern until she faced her insecurity.

What patterns can you see in your break-up history?

When you examine the significant relationships in your life, do you see some pattern developing? If you do, then you can address these and make different choices. Dating, like life, is about making choices. If something isn't working for you, make a different choice. If that choice doesn't work for you, make yet another choice. For any patterns that you saw emerge while doing this exercise, what would you do differently?

CHAPTER 6

Are You Ready to Get in The Game?

There are so many people seeking a committed relationship. You will find millions of people on dating websites, advertising in the personal ads, joining dating services, and becoming members of singles clubs and groups. You obviously want a fulfilling relationship, too. That is why you are reading this book. The question becomes: Why do you want to be in a committed relationship? Have you ever really thought about it? What will a committed relationship give you that you are not currently getting? Can you get that on your own? Are you looking for someone to catapult you to the next level in life? These are tough questions. For your own benefit, answer them honestly.

Readiness Factor

Before we work with a new client, we ask this tough question: So, why do you want to be in a relationship? The Readiness Factor is very important to a person's success in dating and relationships. The answers we received from our clients are fascinating and insightful. We have broken the answers down into categories to help you evaluate your readiness.

The Clock

- I have finished school and have a good job. It is time for marriage.

- I want to have children. My biological clock is ticking.

- My parents want grandchildren.

- All my friends are getting married.

- I've been divorced more than a year. It is time to get back in a relationship.

- We've been dating a long time. The next logical step is marriage.

Do any of these sound remotely familiar? The pressure of a self-imposed time clock can cause people to make relationship choices before they are emotionally ready or for the wrong reasons.

One of our good friends admitted that her first marriage was the result of a self-imposed time clock. She had graduated from college and obtained her teaching credential. It was time to get married and have children. She had this timeline for her whole life. She wanted to be married by twenty-four and have children by twenty-six.

She had dated some really nice men in high school and college. When she left college, "the well" of available men seemed to be drying up. She joined a dating service and was on the quest to meet her future husband. Before she really scratched the surface of using the dating service, she met a man in the parking lot of the local grocery store. They were both in love with the idea of getting married and having a family. There were signs that he was not the right person for her. She saw the red flags but chose to ignore them. The call of the clock was overpowering. She was married by twenty-four, had her daughter at twenty-six and was divorced at twenty-eight.

This is an example of a classic mistake. A question to seriously ponder is: Are you in love with the person or in love with the idea of getting married or being in a relationship?

Surrendering to Loneliness

- I am lonely. I want someone to come home to at night.

- I am tired of dating and the dating game.

- I don't want to be a single mom/dad forever.

- I am bored with being single.

Don't jump from the frying pan into the fire. Being lonely or bored is a huge snare that can trap you into an unfulfilling relationship. In our coaching practice, we have met many married people who were very lonely or bored. Marriage is not the cure for loneliness or boredom. One of the most important steps one must take before entering into marriage is: Being comfortable with being alone. If you are capable of filling your life with experiences that are pleasurable and are happy spending time alone, you are on your way to being ready for a long-term relationship.

We recall a woman telling us how lonely she was in her marriage. She was complaining about her husband working many long hours and then playing golf on the weekends. She wanted him home to spend time with her because she was lonely. The more she complained, the more time he spent away from home. What a surprise! She was asking her husband to fill a void in her life. She wasn't comfortable being alone. Her driving force wasn't her desire to be with her husband and enjoy time with him. Her driving force was not to be lonely. This is a sure way to drive someone away from you. Any healthy relationship needs these three things to prevent this ugly lonely cycle: his time, her time and relationship time. If you don't have interests, hobbies and friendships to fill the time that is slotted for you alone, you are destined to drain your partner's energy by requesting that he/she fill that void.

Being single isn't synonymous with loneliness. Being married isn't an insurance policy against loneliness. We know of many singles who lead extremely active social lives. They consider it a treat just to get some time alone! We also know of married people who have existed for years in a parallel universe with their spouse and are extremely lonely. They live in the same house but have very little connection.

Security, Security, Security

- I am tired of living on my own.

- Two can live as cheaply as one.

- I hate my job. If I get married I can afford to change careers.

- I want to buy a house.

- I want to be a stay-at-home mom.

- I'm pregnant.

- She's pregnant, so I should marry her.

- I want to get out of my parents' house.

- I'm not making enough money to support myself.

- I want to marry someone who makes a lot of money.

- I want to start planning for my financial future with someone.

- With two incomes, we can afford more things in life.

These are actual answers from some of our clients. We were surprised that many people want to get into a committed relationship to enhance their financial situation, standing or status. Marriage is not a business deal. It is a life partnership. Gaining more financial security can be a by-product of a marriage but it is not a reason to get into a long-term committed relationship.

Keith and I have gone through many peaks and valleys financially throughout our marriage. We know that if we lost everything, we would still be fine because we have each other. We truly love each other and are devoted to our marriage. Our financial situation was not what made our marriage successful. Money can make things easier but it does *not* make a marriage.

One of the top reasons people in their twenties and thirties get married is because of an unplanned pregnancy. Often, the fear raising a child on her own can lead a single woman to marry the father of her unborn child although they are not truly compatible as a couple. Many couples in this situation believe that they should get married to provide the child with a stable home. Marriage does not create a stable home. A solid relationship creates a solid home.

If you are not able to support yourself, you are not ready to enter into a relationship. Some people may disagree with us on this point. However, it is our feeling that a relationship has a much greater opportunity for success if each person comes into the relationship having the ability to support one's self. If both parties are able to support themselves before entering into a long-term relationship, you can avoid the pitfall of getting stuck in a relationship for monetary reasons.

If you can't make ends meet financially, get another job or get a better education to improve your earning capacity. If you can't afford to live on your own, get a roommate. Two can live as cheaply as one in a roommate situation too. If you want to buy house and can't afford it on your own, form a partnership with a financially responsible person or group and invest together.

Get married because you love each other and want to spend your life together. Get married because you are a good match for each other. Get married because you love and support each other's dreams and goals and make each other happy!

Self-Esteem

- He/She is the best person I have dated. This is the best I can do.

- If I don't get married, people will think I'm a loser.

- People think he/she is great. I guess I should marry him/her. I could do a lot worse.

- If I don't marry him/her, I might end up alone forever.

- I'm not that great of a catch. I should be happy with him/her.

- I am overweight. There aren't too many good options.

- I'm not attractive to the opposite sex. At least he/she finds me attractive.

Self-esteem issues are one of top reasons people marry the wrong person. They settle for a person because they are afraid that nothing better will come along. Often, they enter a loveless relationship or a relationship where the person mistreats them. Having low self-esteem can set you up in a relationship that is abusive or neglectful.

When we marry, part of the wedding vow is, "until death do us part." You don't want to be wishing for death to come quickly and put you out of your misery. It is important to take the time to heal your self-image. This will make you a much healthier partner in a marriage. You can seek the help of a qualified psychologist or life coach that can help you see yourself in a different light.

No one goes into a relationship wanting it to fail. Relationships fail for many reasons. One of the top reasons for relationships failing is that one or both of the people are not ready.

Previously, we mentioned the line from the movie Jerry McGuire "You complete me!" No relationship will complete you. No relationship will make you completely happy in your life. Going into a relationship wanting someone to make you feel better about yourself is setting the relationship up for big problems and possible failure.

Being in a "soul mate" type relationship is one that feeds the body, mind and spirit. When you are in a soul mate relationship, you don't keep score or track of what your partner is doing for you. You don't give with the anticipation of expecting something in return. You request what you need and just know that your partner will be there for you just like you will be there in return. It is where the depth of the person's love and spirit is the most desirable part of being in a relationship. Your ideal mate will treat you with respect and he/she will be healthy enough to sustain and develop a relationship that is intimate and satisfying for both parties.

The most successful relationships are created when both people feel complete about their own life, and a healthy love relationship is just the icing on the cake. You must be in a relationship with someone who complements your life. Can your relationship be successful if you are unhappy in your life or unhappy with yourself? Yes, but it is kind of like flipping a coin. Wouldn't you be better served to take the time first to choose to be happy with your own life and with yourself?

CHAPTER 7

There is a Yellow Flag on the Field

There are some areas to consider when making a relationship choice that might not be on your radar screen, but definitely should be examined. Remember, that when you are choosing your ideal mate, you are looking for compatibility and commonality. Examine the following areas. If these are important to you, you might want to mark them with a highlighter. They will play a part in creating your ideal mate list later in this book.

Cultural Differences: These differences may or may not be problematic. They may impact the roles the male and female play in the relationship and attitudes about how men and women interact. Understanding the differences and your ability to accept your partner's views must be explored. Often, cultural differences impact extended family relationships as well. The term "culture" has a broad meaning, which can range from people from differing countries to people from different socio-economic backgrounds.

Religious Differences: People who feel strongly about their religious views and upbringing are less flexible than those who are open to exploring other religions and accepting differences. If both people can give the other person the freedom and support to follow their beliefs, there is not a problem. Often, one person will convert to the others religion. In some relationships, both religions are celebrated in the home (i.e. Jewish and Christian.) If you plan to have children, you must discuss what religion the children will follow. It would be best to be with someone with whom you share a religious faith or someone who is tolerant and supportive of you having a different faith and vice versa.

Major Problems (lawsuits, health conditions, etc.): When you get into a relationship, you get the whole package. If there are things that seriously impact your relationship, you must evaluate your willingness to stick things out. Do you want to go into a serious relationship knowing what you already know? Do you love the person enough to stay in the relationship regardless of what might be in store for you both?

If someone has a large financial debt, the minute you say "I DO," you have taken on that debt, too. Are you willing to pay for these bills if a marriage ends? Creditors don't care if he/she pays or you pay. They just want to get paid.

If your partner has been through a difficult divorce and their ex-spouse continues to drag them back to court on a regular basis, are you willing to stand by your man/woman? Are you willing to give love and support through the ongoing turmoil?

Educational or Socioeconomic Differences: The closer the match educationally and socioeconomically, the higher the probability of a successful relationship. Relationships where there are significant educational or socioeconomic differences can work when certain other factors are in place. For instance, you might fall in love with someone who does not have a formal education and you do. But the person is very well read, thus they have created a significant informal education.

You might fall in love with someone who grew up poor but has worked very hard to become financially successful. They want to own a home in a good community, drive a nice car, and take great vacations, etc. You've grown up with all these luxuries. Because of the other person's desire to also have these things, you might have a match.

Different Values: We all have a unique set of values. If your values are polarized with your life partner, then you will have less commonality and a harder time reaching agreement in your relationship. This can impact how you handle money, interact with the world, and raise children. Ideally, partners who share a similar set of core values will have an easier time working out their relationship when times get tough.

Lifestyle Differences: Consider where you might want to live: rural vs. urban/suburban. Do you like dogs and they like cats? She wants two children and you want six. He doesn't want children and she has a burning desire to be a mother. What are the factors that would make your life compatible with your partner? What can you compromise on? Are there deal breakers? Don't go into the relationship thinking you can change your partner's mind later. There are some decisions that should be on the table very early on in the dating process to ensure commonality.

Bad Timing: You can have a great match with someone but the timing is just bad. Stay in contact, but do not put your life on hold. Keep moving forward and dating. If the person becomes available that's great. If they don't, you will not have lost any time waiting for them.

Large Age Difference: The younger you are, the more impact a significant age difference can be on a relationship. Let's say that you are twenty and dating someone who is forty. The potential problems you will face are:

- You will have a different social circle.
- The older you get, the more you will experience an energy and health disparity. When you are fifty, they will be seventy and so on.
- You will have different interests including music, movies and activities.

A good question to ask is, "Am I looking for a role model in my life partner?" If you didn't get a lot of guidance from a parent, you might choose someone older. As you mature, you won't need a role model in your life 24/7. You will need a life partner who supports your emotional growth.

Now, if you are fifty and dating someone who is seventy, you might have similar energy, interests and both of you definitely have more life experience. Take yourself out another ten years. You will be sixty and they will be eighty. Will there be a significant difference in energy and health at this time? Probably! Are you willing to take on the role of care-giver as their health declines? Just some food for thought!

CHAPTER 8

Cupid Throws a Red Flag

If you have been bitten by the Love Bug, you know it. There is no greater natural high than falling in love. The sky seems bluer, the grass greener, the days are sweeter, the songs on the radio are more touching and have new meaning when you are in love.

Have you seen clips of Tom Cruise on the Oprah Winfrey Show during the early months of his relationship with Katie Holmes? He was absolutely giddy. He jumped on the furniture and proclaimed that he was in love. There was no question in our minds that he had been bitten by the Love Bug.

The bite of the Love Bug has some other symptoms as well. The bite can leave you blind to what is really going on in a relationship. It can paralyze your ability to reason. It can also increase your ability to make excuses for yourself and your partner.

There is no cure for the bite of the Love Bug. The effects of being bitten can last three to six months. They call this the honeymoon stage of a relationship. During this period of time, you are not yourself. Trust us! It is important to take things slow during this time, build the relationship and really get to know the person you are dating. If a relationship is suppose to last a lifetime, what is the hurry?

When we fall in love, it is easy to overlook some personality flaws in our potential partners that can be fatal to a relationship. Go into a relationship with your eyes wide open. It is more painful to exit a relationship that is six months old rather than one that is six weeks old.

Recognizing that your lover has a fatal flaw is extremely important, therefore, we are going to outline the thirteen fatal personality traits that will kill love every time! If you discover one or more of the fatal flaws in your lover, we certainly hope you will seriously consider leaving. Remember, you can't fix them by loving them.

Red Flags

Take a look at the following 13 fatal personality trait profiles. While you are reading this chapter, have a pen or pencil in hand. If you have ever been in a relationship with someone who had one of these fatal flaws, jot their name down in the margin of the book. It is possible that someone might have more than one of these fatal flaws. We call this the double-whammy and you are lucky not to be in a relationship with them any longer.

The Commitment Phobic

When people hear the words "commitment phobic," they usually think that we are referring to men. There are a lot of women out there that are just as fearful of commitment. So how do you recognize a person who is a non-committer?

One of the most important things we have discovered from our dating and coaching experiences is that anything quickly attained is more likely than not, quickly lost. Men and/or women who quickly push a relationship forward should trigger a red flag that you need to stop and examine the relationship. This is a sign that you might be with a "commitment phobic" or even an abusive person.

The "commitment phobic" personality presents itself in two very distinct phases. Most commitment phobic people are not conscious of the game they are playing. The first phase of the game is to bait a person into the relationship. The person doing the baiting makes the other person feel special, desired and wanted. They make the other person believe that they are the chosen one. "I have chosen you to be my potential life partner. I love so many things about you."

Now, this may all seem normal in a romantic relationship. If fact, it is highly desired in a love relationship by most people. But there are more signs to spot.

Phase 1: They show a high level of interest in you and come on quite strong. Often they seem vulnerable, showing fear that you might not care about them in the same way.

- They often profess that you just might be that "someone special" and they have set their sights on you.

- They put their very best foot forward, doing everything possible to impress you using their best "dog and pony" and "smoke and mirror" show. They send flowers, cook you a meal or plan a romantic picnic. You know the drill.

- Goes out of his/her way to be with you and stay connected. They call you just to say hello or "I love you." They send you cute text messages.

- They begin to talk about having a future together early in the dating process. The attention from this person can feel overwhelming but wonderful at the same time.

- They profess their desire to have a meaningful monogamous relationship through words and actions.

- Despite their rocky relationship history, they lead you to believe that this relationship will be different because you are just so special.

When a woman showers a man with this level of attention, many men head for the hills. However, there are some men who are flattered by the attention. They also feel empowered by someone who is willing to dance and sing his/her way into their heart.

Women tend to buy into these behaviors from men hook, line and sinker. It is nice to have someone interested in you. Women are more motivated to find a mate and unknowingly put the blinders on. They become emotionally invested early in the relationship and can't see that these behaviors may be problematic.

If the person is not a serial dater or commitment phobic, we are still going to wave a big red flag. A person who shows these behaviors is potentially quite needy and insecure.

Another even bigger red flag is that the behaviors described above are also some of the classic signs of an abuser! The abuser will suck you in with their sweetness and attentiveness. However, their calls and text messages are a way to keep tabs on you. They want to be with you all the time because then they know where you are. They begin to isolate you from your friends and family because this gives them more opportunity to make their moves. Almost anyone can maintain a good impression for a few months. However, an abuser cannot control his or her good behavior for any extended period of time. Therefore, they want to seal the deal before you find out that they have major faults. They want a relationship in which they are in control.

Now, let's take a look at the second phase of the "commitment phobic's" behavior. This is where the real trouble begins.

Phase 2: Let the criticisms begin. They are highly critical of you and/ or the relationship as a whole. (This is also a classic sign of an abusive person. Don't walk away from the relationship ... RUN!!!!)

- Their actions begin to sabotage the relationship. Where they were attentive early in the relationship, they begin showing signs of "I'm really not that into you." They are late for dates or cancel them often. They appear to be busy and unavailable. They may be very apologetic but it keeps happening. The sabotaging may show up in a number of ways but you keeping getting disappointed, hurt or annoyed by the behavior.

- They begin saying things like "I am feeling like our relationship is taking over my life." "You are too needy." "I need some space."

- The talk about a future together slows down drastically or stops all together. Any discussion that indicates making a commitment or any forward movement (moving in together, getting engaged, and marriage) is avoided or ends up in a fight. Often they throw out roadblocks like: "If you weren't so_____, maybe I would be more open to talking about a future together."

- Where they once worshiped the ground you walked on, now they find fault in you and make you feel like you will never measure up.

- The yo-yo relationship is also another indicator. They leave the relationship and then return to the relationship again and again if you keep letting them come back. Because they know you will let them back in your life, they have no reason to commit.

If you see these signs in your relationship, say next! You deserve to find someone who wants to be with you. Your ideal mate will love you with all your warts. Some *"Commitment Phobic"* people can be tamed but be smart. Why invest years in a very slim possibility?

Recently, a beautiful woman approached us seeking advice about her current relationship. She had been with a man for seven years who was separated from his wife but had never filed for divorce. To top things off, the woman had caught this man on a date with another woman. He swears that this was the only time he dated someone else. She had threatened to leave the relationship several times if he didn't divorce his wife but he always talked her into staying. She was so in love with him and wanted to know how she could get him to commit to the relationship. We asked her if she was willing to leave the relationship. She said no. She was disappointed to learn that we didn't believe there was any way to get this man to commit.

Let's get real here. This woman has low self-esteem. She has tolerated a lack of commitment and infidelity for seven years. She is in love with a "commitment phobic," a man who is not available, not to mention, a cheater. Why should he commit? He is getting his cake and eating it, too. She is not willing to leave and he knows it.

So, how do you smoke out the commitment phobic? Ask for space and tell them that the relationship is moving at a pace faster than what you are comfortable with. Back off and see what behavior follows.

- If they respect your need to take things slowly and are willing to work on building the relationship at a pace that is right for you, you might have a gem. They are a bit insecure, but a diamond in the rough.

- If they begin to sulk and behave like a scolded child, run for the hills. The relationship is all about them and your needs are secondary.

- If they agree to give you space, but continue the same behaviors, just in a more covert way, get out of the relationship. This is a major red flag. Not only is the relationship all about them, they are manipulative, too.

You can spend years and years trying to get a "commitment phobic" to settle down. You are better off finding someone who really wants to be in a relationship. More importantly, you need to find someone who truly does value you as person.

The Abuser

Abuse in a relationship is a slow insidious process. If you started dating someone and on the second or third date they call you a "bitch" or "asshole" early in the relationship, or slapped you, or insulted you verbally, you would bolt for the door. At least we certainly hope you would.

Abuse starts out slowly and builds as time progresses. It might start out with a level of controlling behavior. "You aren't going to wear that, are you?" You go in and change your clothes into another outfit hoping to please your partner. He/she has won the first battle. You buckled. Now that they know you will, they will begin to escalate and increase their controlling behavior.

We once heard this great story about a woman who dated a man who had criticized what she was wearing and wanted her to change her outfit. She didn't. The next time they were going on a date, she called him up and said, "I'm wearing Express jeans, a red long sleeve t-shirt with a V-neckline and red shoes. I wanted you to know because if you don't want to see me in this outfit, don't come over. This is what I am wearing and you are never to tell me what to wear again. Understand?" Wow! How powerful is that? Someone who has the need to control won't win with this girl!

Jeannine Recalls Dating a Potential Abuser

I dated a man who was a delight on the first three dates. The day after our fourth date, he called me. He told me that he was bothered because I was too friendly to our waitress. He felt I should pay more attention to him I mulled this over in my head and thought I should pay attention to this. After our fifth date, I got another call. He told me that he was upset because I didn't tell him how much I enjoyed the date. A light bulb went on in my head. This was a pattern of behavior. I decided to avoid his calls and not date him again. Now, I understand that this was not a very direct or mature way of dealing with the situation. Eventually, he finally got me on the phone and asked why I wouldn't return his calls. I came clean. I told him that I wasn't going to date him anymore. I was tired of the phone calls criticizing me after our dates. He begged for another date. I said "No." He wanted to be friends. I did something wonderful and courageous. I told him that I didn't need a friend who put me down and found faults in me at every turn. We never spoke again.

This was a huge turning point in my dating life. I reclaimed my own value. I deserved to find someone that loved all my wonderful qualities, including my gregarious personality. An abuser can only abuse someone who has low self-esteem. If you think your self-esteem is low now, imagine how low it will be after dating an abuser for six months.

Another sign of abuse is isolation. The abuser begins to isolate you from your friends and family. You might hear things like: "I don't like your friends. They just like to party." He/she might say something like, "Your family is interfering in our relationship. If you want to be with me, you won't discuss our relationship with them." Once the abuser separates you from your support system, they can take control.

Abuse is not a male trait. There are lots of female abusers out there. Violence on any level is not okay. Pushing, shoving, choking, hitting, kicking, pulling hair or physically intimidating a person is not acceptable. Verbal and emotional abuse damages your self-esteem and relationship. No one deserves to be yelled at, called names, or belittled. The bruises from emotional and verbal abuse last a very long time on someone's heart.

The infamous, "I'm sorry" doesn't cut it when it comes to abuse. The person needs help and you need to move on. Don't turn back because they plead or offer an explanation. One of an abuser's number one lines is, "It won't happen again." The only way you can guarantee this is to leave. The first time emotional, verbal or physical abuse happens, leave and seek help. Abuse is a deal killer in any relationship.

The Player or Serial Dater

People who are just looking to have fun or for a sexual partner are energetically coming from a different place than people who are looking for a long-term committed relationship. By not being emotionally invested in the relationship a person is less likely to get hurt if it doesn't work out. We often refer to these people as "players." "Player" is a derogatory term in dating circles, not because it is wrong, but because "players" often aren't honest about being a "player."

If you are involved with a serial dater, chances are that you will pursue him/her vigorously. People want what they can't have. If you are interested in a long-term relationship don't waste your time with a serial dater. Find someone who is interested in a long-term relationship and stop wasting your precious time and energy.

If you are seeking a relationship that is long-term, you need to weed out the "players" early in the dating process. How do you know whether they are a "player" or not? In the process of dating you notice:

- They have a dating history void of committed relationships.

- They don't ask questions about where you want to be in your life.

- They don't include you in their life, friendships and family.

- The relationship isn't shaping up.

- You are doing most of the work in setting up dates.

- You are often waiting for them to call or call you back.

- You get the feeling that they really aren't that into you.

- They frequently cancel dates.

- They frequently call at the last minute and want you to do something. (They have nothing better to do.)

- You see each other infrequently, mostly because they are too busy with "this and that."

We bet some of you can see that these warning signals were present in some of your dating experiences. The challenge isn't that these things are happening, it is ignoring that they are happening. Remember, if you aren't getting your needs met in the honeymoon period of developing a relationship, you certainly won't get them met later. Also, someone's current and past behavior is a great indicator of future behavior. Are you willing to settle for less than you deserve?

The Cheater

If you are dating someone who is in another relationship, how can you trust that he/she won't do the same to you? We are talking about someone's character. When someone wants to set up another relationship before leaving the other, they lack guts. Don't you want to have someone who has the guts to fix the relationship or end the relationship? You don't want to be wondering if your partner is out shopping for a new partner. If that was their mode of operation in one relationship, there is a much higher chance that they will do it again. Past behavior is a great indicator of future behavior.

How many broken hearts have there been because of cheating? More than we can count. If someone cheats, someone is going to get hurt. The chances are high that it will be you if you are dating a cheater. Are you willing to settle for someone who lacks character? Trust is a huge part of a healthy long-term relationship. If you start out in a place where trust has been broken, what kind of faithful, successful, relationship do you expect? You have to be able to trust them.

We need to define what is "single." That might seem like a simple thing, but you would be surprised at how many people struggle with the concept of the term "single." Why date a person who is unavailable? If your goal is to find yourself in a committed relationship, start with someone who has the ability to commit. It is really quite simple to define.

- If they are in another relationship, they are unavailable.

- If they are recently separated and they haven't completed the process of physically and emotionally uncoupling, they are unavailable.

- If they are married, they are unavailable.

- If they are having sex with someone else, they are unavailable.

Remember, you are seeking a long-term committed relationship. If you find yourself in a relationship with someone who is unavailable, you owe it to yourself to tell them you can't continue to see them. If they leave their current partner you might be interested in pursuing a relationship. You should not be interested in a relationship with someone who can't give you his/her whole heart.

The Opposite

A theory in the dating world is that opposites attract. But it is our belief that opposites attract in some situations. If two individuals are seeking a partner to strengthen their weaknesses, they sometimes come together in a relationship. Unfortunately, if the couple does not have a great deal of commonality in their relationship, there is a greater probability that the relationship will fail.

If you are bad with money, you might seek out someone who is fiscally responsible. You may choose a partner who makes solid investments, saves for the future, and sticks to a budget. You might feel that this partner will balance you out. Your shortcoming will not be cured by marrying someone who is good with money. More than likely, you will have some serious arguments about your spending habits and his/her tight grip on their wallet.

We have a friend who married a man who was considerably more socially reserved than she. In the early years of their relationship, it allowed her to shine in a social situation. They went to parties and events, she fluttered around like a social butterfly and he was comfortable being a wallflower. As the relationship progressed, he no longer wanted to go to parties. He was happy staying home. They had many fights about his "anti-social" stance. They began to grow apart and the marriage ended in divorce.

You don't have to be two peas in a pod, but the closer the match, the higher the chance you have for success in a long-term relationship.

The Liar

A healthy relationship is built on honesty, trust and mutual respect. If you are in a relationship with a liar, you won't have any of the cornerstones for a long-term relationship.

People lie for a lot of reasons. Most people lie because they fear they will experience more pain if they tell the truth. They are trying to hide something they said, did or did not do. Sometimes people lie to get something they want. People may lie to make people think they are something or someone they are not. If someone tells enough lies it becomes easy to fall into the habit of lying about everything.

Let's examine the different forms of lying:

- One is the outright lie. There is no truth in their statement or story.

- Another form of lying is the omission of information. This is where the person tells a portion of the truth and then leaves out anything that might be considered unfavorable.

- "Little white lies" usually involve superficial things. People use "little white lies" when they feel the truth would hurt someone's feelings. For example: telling another friend that a haircut looks good when you don't really like it is a "little white lie." Telling your partner that you are on a weekend getaway with a friend when you are having an affair is NOT a "little white lie."

- Some people embellish a story. If he gave his girlfriend a rose, he might tell others that he sent her a dozen long stem roses. If she got a raise, she might tell people that she got a big promotion. A person who is insecure has a tendency to embellish because they want others to see them in a more favorable light. These are still lies.

If your partner lies to other people, they will lie to you. Don't think that love will cure a liar. If you don't have trust and honesty, you don't have a solid foundation for a relationship.

One huge mistake people make is not confronting their partner when they observe him/her lying to someone. If honesty is important to you (and it should be), why tolerate lying from your partner on any level? If you hear them lying or catch them in a lie, don't brush it under the carpet.

A friend of mine was dating a man who had a habit of lying to people quite often. Sometimes he would outright lie. Sometimes he would mislead someone. For instance, if someone misunderstood something he said to them, and it was more favorable to him, he would fail to correct them and would just let them continue thinking that. (This is omission of information.)

This man lied to his mother all the time. One time, he was going on a weekend get-away with his girlfriend. He asked his mother to take care of his cat while he was gone for a few days. His mother assumed that it was a business trip. He allowed her to believe that it was a business trip. Later this man wanted his girlfriend to cover for him and not   discuss their weekend get-away in front of his mother. Our friend didn't like covering up the lie, but she did. (This is omission of information and the conspiracy to continue the lie.)

Her action of accepting the lie set up a pattern of behavior in their relationship. He lied, she covered it up. Eventually, she couldn't trust him anymore. If he could easily lie to others, he was probably lying to her. She began to wonder if he was really on a business trip when he said he was. When he cancelled a date to work late, she wondered if he was out at the clubs with his friends or another woman.

Trust is the foundation of every good relationship. If you are a liar, you need to clean it up. You won't have any quality relationships until you do. If you are in a relationship with a person who lies, you have to actively confront the issue. If you don't, you are passively negotiating that lying is okay in your relationship. If they continue to lie, move on. You deserve better!

The Bad Reputation

If the person you are dating has a reputation for things you find distasteful, there may be fire where you smell smoke. If you think that your love will change them, we have news for you it won't! If you think that you are the exception to the rule and that he/she will not mistreat you, you are being a fool.

If you hear stories about their past and it includes things like violence, aggression, excessive drinking and partying, scanty work history or mistreating others, it is in your best interest to move on. Don't make excuses for their behavior.

Often, people think that they can change someone; love will prevail. You are looking for a long-term, committed relationship. You want a relationship that is healthy from the get go. If you are choosing relationships with people you hope to fix, then you aren't getting that healthy relationship you desire.

We were working with a woman who fell in love with a man who spent more time on unemployment and disability than he had spent time earning an honest day's pay. When he was down to his last few hundred dollars, he would start looking for work. He had many disagreements with his bosses who didn't appreciate his hard work and contribution to the company. He had more jobs in a year than most people have in a lifetime. She felt that he just had a string of bad luck. If she was there for him, he would find the job he loved and everything would be okay.

The reality was, this man could not and would not take responsibility for anything in his life. It was always someone else's fault that he was unsuccessful in his job and in the world. This was not a secret. This woman knew this about him. People in their circle of friends use to joke about it and take bets on how long he would stay on a job before quitting or getting fired. There were smoke signals all over the place.

If you want to be miserable, you can choose someone who needs fixing. Here is an analogy: You can choose a relationship that is like a model home. It is great from the beginning. You can also choose a fixer upper. If you do, be prepared to spend a lot of time at the "Relationship Home Depot."

The Insecure

People who have abandonment issues can be quite smothering. No matter how much you assure them of your love for them and want to be with them, they believe that you have one foot out the door due to their insecurities. You will be exhausted reassuring this person that you are not leaving.

Their mother/father might have left them when they were young.

Their wife/husband may have left them for someone else. These might be real issues they need to deal with. It is not your job to fix them.

Someone who needs constant reassuring that you care about them and want to be with them is not datable. You might think it is cute that they care about you so much, but that will get old really fast. More often than not, a person with abandonment issues or other issues causing deep insecurity will become controlling. They will always want to know when you are coming back. How long will you be gone? Can they come with you? If you are late coming home from work, all hell might break loose!

Can you feel the stress starting to build just from reading about these kinds of people? You will be smothered in no time flat. You will begin finding reasons not to come home so you can have some time to yourself.

Let them get the help they need and get ready to be in a healthy relationship. You need to move on and find someone who is healthy now. Don't feel guilty. You didn't create their problem. By leaving you might be giving them just the incentive they need to go seek some help.

The Partier

We've all met a few partiers in our lifetime. Sometimes we love to be around this person because they are the life of the party. But put up a red flag if you are dating someone who gets high or intoxicated at almost every party or function. This is a sign of a problem. Remember, this person could be the future mother or father of your children. What behaviors do you want in a parent role? If you think that marriage will change the behavior, it won't. Some people outgrow this party phase, but many don't. If you are a partier yourself, you need to get it in check. Are you looking for a future mate or a drinking buddy?

People who get high or intoxicated regularly have a problem. They are, more often than not, an alcoholic or substance abuser. Just because they can keep other parts of their life functioning while partying, doesn't mean they don't have a problem. Alcoholics and drug addicts often can hold their lives together for quite some time. This is another example of the "model home" versus the "fixer upper" relationship. You might be able to put a Band-Aid on the cancer of addiction for quite some time, but eventually the relationship will need some intense chemotherapy.

The Green–Eyed Monster

Jealousy can kill a relationship faster than a cheetah chasing its lunch. At first, jealousy might seem cute and endearing. One might think that the jealous person loves you so much that they don't want to risk losing you to someone else. As time passes, it can become an obsession. People who are jealous are insecure. No amount of reassuring can tame the green-eyed monster of jealousy.

We all have a bit of jealousy in us. It is normal. When jealousy becomes a pattern and negatively impacts a relationship, it is a problem. If someone tells you that they were a bit jealous that so-and-so was talking with you, slight jealousy should not be a problem unless it happens several (meaning two or more) times. That is when your radar needs to go up.

Just because someone else cheated on them does not give someone the license to become jealous or controlling. If you allow this to happen, you are making a very big mistake. Why should you do the time for someone else's crime?

Jealousy can grow. He/She might not want you out of their sight. They think anyone who is nice to you is flirting with you. They want to know where you are at every minute. They might even check up on you and drop by your friend's home to make sure you are really there. Your privacy will become invaded. It is not unheard of to have the "Green-Eyed Monster" riffle through your cell phone log, your personal belongings, your car and wallet. In fact, this kind of behavior is common among jealous people. They may even follow you when you go somewhere or place a GPS tracking device in your car. Sound like prison? It can be!

Self-Deprecating Soul

Low self-esteem is not always apparent. However, those who make statements that include the following are clearly suffering from low self-esteem:

- I don't deserve someone like you. You are a better person than me.

- I'm a screw-up.

- I'm just not very successful in life. I try really hard but I just don't seem to do things right.

- I have the job skills to be successful but I am competing in the job market with people who are more outgoing and more attractive. It is hard to be successful.

- Stay away from me, I am trouble.

- You won't like me once you really know me or see my dark side.

Our tendency is to reassure the self-deprecating soul by pointing out all the positive qualities we see in them. Your praise will fall on deaf ears because, this type of person uses self-deprecation to make people feel sorry for them and to keep from being criticized. The self-deprecating soul has learned that most loving people won't criticize someone who already feels bad and has low self-esteem. Therefore, you will find yourself in a relationship where you cannot express your disappointment in your partner for fear that it will further destroy his/her fragile self image.

Freeloader

This person often appears to have a string of bad luck. They lose their jobs, can't find a job, or lost their apartment, etc. This seems to be a pattern in their life. They are a lost person who doesn't seem to have control over their life. They make people feel sorry for them or use their charm to get others to take care of them until they get on their feet (which they almost never do). They may look to you for every kind of support including financial. He/She is looking for someone else to take care of them. In fact, they will likely reject you if you do not take care of them. They are not a responsible adult and are therefore, not partner material.

The Blamer

This person blames others for the failings in their life. Of course, what happens to them is never their fault, but "blamers" are unable to take responsibility for their part of a relationship failing. When things go wrong at work, it is not because of something they did or did not do. It is always someone else's fault, or someone is just being hard on them. They fail to take responsibility for their actions or feelings. They often cannot or will not say "I am sorry" or "I was wrong or mistaken." When you are in a relationship with the "blamer," you will continually have to bite your tongue to keep the peace.

The more positive your self-esteem, the less likely you are to fall prey to one of the fatal flaw profiles. That is why we wrote this book with the emphasis focusing on you! Raising your self-esteem and awareness will decrease the likelihood that you will put up with someone mistreating you in any way. You will be more apt to ask them to leave your life and not let the door hit him/her on the way out.

By looking at your relationship beliefs, you will have a greater ability to identify some patterns that might feel "normal" to you but that you don't want in your ideal love relationship. For instance, if you come from an abusive home, when someone says something hurtful or negative, you might not immediately identify that this is not okay. Even though these words hurt you, it might feel familiar. The more you can get in touch with your relationship beliefs and patterns, the more likely you are to wake up and start setting boundaries, including leaving destructive relationships early. Claim that your ideal mate will not mistreat you. Anyone who does mistreat you gets the boot!

Step into your "deservingness." Deservingness is not a word you will find in the dictionary. It is our new word. The more deserving you feel of having someone in your life to treat you well, the less you will accept behaviors that are contrary to that desire.

EXERCISE: Your Red Flags

Re-examine the above 13 fatal personality trait profiles. Have you ever been in a relationship with someone with one or more of these flaws? If so, how were you feeling about yourself when you got involved in the relationship? Write down any of the flaws identified below that you have seen in past partners or any that may ring true with you. Later in the book, we will be making your ideal mate relationship list. Fatal flaws will be an important "don't want" on your list. You will then convert this "don't want" into what you want instead. Now that you are aware of the fatal personality traits, you are in a much better position to avoid them and find a healthy love partner.

CHAPTER 9

Game Stopping Relationship Patterns

Relationship patterns are simply that–patterns. But, some of these patterns can actually kill your opportunity to find love. We call these *Toxic Relationship Patterns* and we strongly encourage you to become aware of the toxic choices you have made in your past so, you can make better, healthier choices in the future.

You may choose these relationships patterns for different reasons, but most often people make these relationship choices because they need two things:

First is the need to heal old wounds. Sometimes these are wounds from our childhood and others are from the experiences of painful love relationships.

The second reason we choose *Toxic Relationship Patterns* is our attempt to increase our self-worth. Sometimes, you choose a relationship with someone who needs a life make-over and you are just the person who can help them. Other times, you choose someone you can place on a pedestal and attempt to raise your self-worth by being more like them.

Earlier in this book, we made it clear that no one can complete you. But you can be in a relationship with someone whom you honor and who honors you. If you choose a *Toxic Relationship Pattern*, it will be impossible for you to achieve this goal. These patterns are an attempt to fill a hole within you! No one can fill that hole. Only YOU can do that for YOU!

By identifying the *Toxic Relationship Patterns* you have engaged in thus far, you can begin to shift to healthier choices and begin to heal your wounds.

There are ten primary *Toxic Relationship Patterns*. You may find that you have chosen one pattern or several patterns. Each pattern will be laid out for you to examine in this chapter. Additionally, we will reveal the most common reasons for choosing each of these patterns.

Here are the top 10 *Toxic Relationship Patterns* you want to avoid:

Toxic Relationship Pattern #1: *You are more invested in the relationship than your partner.*

The easiest way to identify that you are engaged in this relationship pattern is by acknowledging that you are doing most of the work to keep the relationship alive. You are the person who is keeping the relationship going by calling, texting, planning activities, doing cute romantic things but getting very little in return. You initiate signs of affection like a kiss, hug, holding hands and even sex. When he/she initiates signs of affection, it is usually as a prelude to having sex.

You are more excited about the relationship than your partner. You think about them all the time when you are apart, but they seem to be just fine without you. You work your life around their schedule and availability but they seem to do little to accommodate your time.

You get just enough back to keep you baited into believing that the other person will return your feelings soon. Your love interest will eventually see what a great catch you are and fall madly in love with you!

The reason for choosing this type of relationship is often tied to a low self-esteem. You believe that your value as a person is tied to what you "do" and not who you "are." You have to prove your value through your actions and what you are willing to give the other person.

Often, the attention you got as a child was directly tied to how well you did in sports, school or displaying a talent. There was little or no reinforcement around you, the person. So, you have drawn the conclusions that "what you do" determines how much you are loved.

Being loved because you are just a good person is foreign to you, so you seek relationships that recreate what you know. You give, give, and give, hoping to eventually get acknowledged and loved.

Most of these relationships end with the other person seeking and getting into another relationship; often while they are still in relationship with you. This results in making you believe that you didn't do enough, you weren't worthy of being loved, and a vicious cycle begins. Your feeling of unworthiness leads you to do more in the next relationship and the pattern repeats itself.

You might be recreating the relationship between your mother and father and are playing the role of the parent who got little or no attention from the other partner. This parent accepted and received the left-over time and energy of their partner and it was clear that they weren't a priority in their spouse's life.

Toxic Relationship Pattern #2: *They are more invested in the relationship than you.*

You know that you aren't as into your partner as he/she is into you. But, you stay because you would rather be with someone than no one. You are defensive when you are accused of not giving them enough attention and you feel pressured to give more. You feel you should be giving more, but you don't have this burning desire to spend more time with them. You know they are a good, loving and giving person but there just is not any magic for you. The more they request your time and attention, the more you withdraw feeling claustrophobic because of their neediness and clinginess.

You might be repeating a pattern you observed between your parents. It could be that your father traveled a lot during your childhood and was not available emotionally or didn't make time for your mother. Your father was putting his attention on his work, the children, friendships, extended family or his personal interests. This is how you think a couple should interact. It feels foreign to you to be in a relationship where the couple interacts emotionally and physically. Therefore, you withdraw.

The second thing that may be rearing its ugly head in this situation is that you don't feel deserving of someone who showers you with attention. You don't know how to let it in, so you choose to not to engage. In a sense, you are punishing yourself because you don't feel enough self-worth to receive. You actually gravitate to relationships that are emotionally bankrupt, not loving, giving, healthy relationships.

Toxic Relationship Pattern #3: *The Fixer Upper: If you love them enough, you can fix them.*

This is one of those "relationship Home Depot projects." You have fallen in love with their potential, not them. He/She just needs more time so you take them on as a project. You tell yourself that no one has loved them enough to overcome their emotional scars and you make excuses to your family and friends for your partner and his/her behavior. Your belief is: If they knew him/her as well as I know him/her, they would understand why I love him/her.

Most of the time, you see their emotional scars, but they don't. What is worse, sometimes they do see their emotional scars, but they have no desire to heal their wounds. This is like buying a fixer-upper home. You see the potential of the home. Spackle the holes in the walls, put on a coat of paint, throw up some new curtains, refinish the floors and you have a terrific home. But, your partner looks at the home and says, "I can live with it this way." Or they might tell you that they are willing to spackle, paint and refinish, but when you buy the products to do the work, these products sit in the garage gathering dust. Sound frustrating?

Falling in love with "a project" will be unfulfilling. So why do people choose this type of relationship? The most common reason is because they don't believe that the "model home" man or woman would fall in love with them. So they choose the fixer-upper and try to turn them into the "model home" partner.

Most people who choose this *Toxic Relationship Pattern* have grown up in an environment where they felt that they were "not enough." You brought home a report card that was nearly straight "A's" but your parents focused on the "B" on your report card. You made the football team, but you weren't the star quarterback. You are in the school play, but you weren't playing the lead role. You did a great job cleaning your room, but you didn't vacuum around the edges of the room. You were constantly being compared to your more talented or intelligent sibling. Your relationships with your parents were demanding and controlling. You finally accept that you will never be enough.

By taking on a project, you get to avoid facing your own life. After all, this project is so much more important. You are "more" than your partner. Finally, you have the upper hand. You might also feel like you are in control by choosing a "fixer upper." You have it more together than your partner and, therefore, get to call the shots.

Toxic Relationship Pattern #4: *You put them on a pedestal.*

You choose someone who is smarter or more successful than you. They seem to have it all together. You look up to them, and even place them on a pedestal. They gladly climb up on the pedestal, glowing in your admiration. You seek your partner's advice and follow it almost blindly. You often quote your partner as if they are an authority on many subjects. You replace you own judgment with your partner's judgment, even when they are frequently wrong.

In this type of relationship, it easy to lose a sense of yourself. The longer you are in this type of relationship, the more you begin to question your ability to make decisions.

It is healthy to admire and respect your partner, but you have to admire and respect yourself, too. If you don't respect yourself, you are dead in the water. If you are with a partner who doesn't respect and admire you, you are headed for some choppy waters.

People who choose this type of relationship either came from a home where there was little or no guidance. They long for someone to be the guiding light in their life. Sometimes, people choose this type of relationship because they were raised by controlling parents who made all of the decisions for them from their friends, to what sports they participated in. If this was you, you may have blindly followed your parents' wishes. When you finally got out on your own, you questioned your ability to make good decisions. So you replaced your parents with a partner who is an authority figure.

Toxic Relationship Pattern #5: *You rebellously choose a partner that gets under your parents' skin.*

The more distasteful your partner is to your parents, the more pleasure you derive from being in the relationship.

You grew up in a strict Catholic home and even went to Catholic school. You only date men/women outside of your religion. An atheist is even better. As long as they get the hair on the back of your father's/mother's neck to stand up, this works for you.

It could be that your father is a conservative white man. You only date women of color knowing that it will make him uncomfortable.

The more he squirms, the more pleasure you derive.

Your parents have urged you to marry a man who is financially stable. Instead, you date men who are unemployed or financially irresponsible.

You are attempting to exert your independence by making bold statements through your selection of a mate. You have to learn to claim your independence without sabotaging your relationships. If you don't, you might end up marrying someone you don't really love, respect or admire just to "show them." In the end, you--not your parents are going to be the one living with your choice.

Toxic Relationship Pattern #6: *Choosing a partner who is the complete opposite of your previous relationship.*

We call this making a wide swing. When one type of partner doesn't work out, you choose someone at the opposite side of the pendulum. If you dated someone who was super controlling, you might date someone with no backbone at all. If you dated someone who was very conservative, you might choose someone who is very untraditional and marches to the beat of a different drummer. If your partner was sexually reserved, you might choose a partner who is a wild adventurous sex addict. The point we are making is you must be aware of the potential to make a very wide swing to the extreme opposite.

The opposite isn't what you need, but it is a knee-jerk reaction to a failed love affair. If you had taken the time to examine what would have served you better, you would have chosen someone in between. By reacting in this extreme manner, you are setting yourself up for more heartache and disappointment.

Toxic Relationship Pattern #7: *Choosing unavailable partners.*

A person who chooses to become involved with someone who

is married, engaged, in a committed relationship or having sex with another partner is choosing unavailable partners. He/She is willing to take the leftover scraps of time, energy and attention in hopes that their partner will pick them over the other person. Often, it is because they were neglected by one or both of their parents. Being in a relationship with a partner who is unavailable actually feels normal.

Someone who chooses this type of relationship has a fear of intimacy or commitment. Often, they have been abused, molested or raped. Keeping her/his distance in a relationship is a protective stance. If they choose to be involved with someone who is in another relationship, then he/she doesn't have to get close. Their partner's emotional needs are being met by someone else, too.

This type of relationship is bound to cause pain, both during the relationship and when it ends. If you choose this type of relationship, you owe it to yourself to make some different choices. Make it a personal policy not to date ANYONE who is unavailable. Tell the person that you would love to date them if and when they end their current relationship. If you are in a relationship now with an unavailable person, end it! Tell them that you are willing to revisit the relationship if they leave their partner, but not before.

Toxic Fatal Relationship Pattern #8: *Being the super hero and rescuing your partner.*

Choosing someone who needs help in any way allows you the right to wear the title of Rescue-holic in your life. Don't confuse sympathy with love. If someone is ill (mentally or physically) and needs you, it is not a reason to get into a relationship. You might get into a relationship with someone who is down on their financial luck and needs to get back on his/her feet. Showering them with endless checks from your open checkbook is not a sign of love. It is a sign of stupidity.

If someone has lost their job and you spend countless hours helping them look for a new one, you are attempting to rescue them.

Because of your need to rescue, you might choose someone with health issues. You step in and take them to doctor appointments, you investigate alternative medicine to treat aliments and help him/her find healthier ways of living to ease the sickness. These are signs that you are falling into the Rescue-holic trap.

Your partner must be willing to take responsibility for his/her own life and health. You might feel like a white knight or an angel of mercy who comes in and rescues someone from the harshness of their life and takes care of him/her. This is not the foundation of a quality relationship. Once you allow yourself to get sucked into being the white knight or the rescue angel, it is rather difficult to leave because you will feel like you are abandoning him/her.

People don't typically go looking for a person to rescue but their need to feel noble and helpful can send them on this destructive course. If you need to be the angel of mercy, get a dog from the pound, volunteer at the food bank, become a mentor, big brother or big sister. But don't look for a love relationship that "needs you." A healthy relationship requires give and take.

Toxic Relationship Pattern #9: *Mistaking your attraction to their looks or talents for love.*

A few years ago, one of our friends fell madly in love with a woman's long and shiny jet black hair. He couldn't stop talking about it. He talked about how it looked, how it smelled and how the sun caught the color. After a month of dating, he became very disillusioned when he realized that he had nothing in common with this woman. She was egotistical, vain and as dumb as a box of rocks.

We can fall for physical characteristics like someone's piercing blue eyes, supermodel legs, or their dazzling smile. But that physical quality can leave us feeling empty when it comes to sustaining a long term relationship.

Jeannine remembers falling for the star of a water ski show at a local theme park. She didn't know anything about him but she was infatuated by his talent and stardom. It took her about a month to realize that he was a total jerk but for that month, she thought she was falling in love.

Another man Jeannine dated wrote her an enchanting love song that he performed on stage at one of his concerts. He was a two-bit singer in a two-bit band, but this love song sucked her in. She didn't need anything else. He was so romantic. Months later, she came to realize that she was in love with his musical talent, not him.

Relationships that begin with superficial infatuation usually don't last long. How long can you stare into those piercing blue eyes or run your fingers through that long silky hair before you get bored? From our personal experiences of falling in love with the external--it doesn't last long!

Toxic Relationship Pattern #10: *Basing an entire relationship on a single common experience.*

We once counseled a woman who had fallen in love with a very attractive and engaging man at her place of work. He seemed to know exactly what she was thinking. He appreciated all her ideas. When she had worked with him on a project, she felt special, brilliant and appreciated. She confused this feeling with love and compatibility. The truth was, outside of this project, they had very little in common. Solely based on euphoric feelings they both derived from this shared work, they launched into a love relationship which failed miserably.

Another common partial compatibility mistake people make is meeting someone on vacation and confusing the torrid love affair with falling in love. You are in a romantic setting, free of the stress of everyday life and you meet someone. There are intimate dinners, shared experiences of visiting the tourist attractions and vacation sex. Then you are back to the real world. When you try to continue the relationship, you realize that you have very little in common. You didn't explore your overall compatibility because you were so caught up in the romance of the vacation.

Don't get swept away by the feelings that can emerge from sharing a common experience. It is easy to confuse these feeling with falling in love.

EXERCISE: Stop! Examine Your Relationship Patterns

Are you falling into Toxic Relationship Patterns? Is one more dominant than the others? If so, take some time to think about the "why" behind this choice. Address the "why" in order to enter healthy relationships.

People who choose Toxic Relationship Patterns are usually lacking self-love. They are willing to put up with someone's bad behavior because they are afraid that they can't do any better. The fear of loneliness that if they leave the relationship is stronger than their desire to be in a healthy relationship. Understand that if you continue to choose Toxic Relationship Patterns, you are choosing PAIN!

If you acknowledge that you have been choosing Toxic Relationship Patterns, go back to Chapter Two, Falling in Love with You and do all the exercises. You also might consider seeing a counselor who can help you raise your self-esteem. You'll be glad you did.

CHAPTER 10

You Are Out of Bounds!

Now that you have a clear picture of the men, women and the relationships to avoid, the next area to explore is setting boundaries, not only in your love life but in your whole life.

As an adult, you are solely responsible for establishing your own personal boundaries and to make your boundaries clear to someone who is violating your emotional or physical space, or well-being. We'll go even further and say that you have an obligation to yourself. You are the most precious thing in your life. Setting and maintaining healthy boundaries is a big step in establishing that you are important. We teach others how to treat us. Without establishing boundaries, you are teaching others that they can walk all over you and without accepting any consequences.

Think for a moment about your most prized possession. It might be a piece of jewelry, your car, or a family heirloom. How do you take care of that special thing? Do you keep it in a special place? Do you make sure that it is clean and well-cared for so you can maintain its importance or beauty? Well, YOU are more important than any coveted prized-possession in your life. If you don't value yourself, how can you expect others to value you as well? Setting boundaries tells the world that YOU value YOU and they should, too!

Learning to set boundaries is a challenging area in our coaching practice. We have found that many men and women lack the skills to set proper boundaries in their lives. Women seem to have more trouble than men because women have been taught to "play nice!"

When we work with someone who has boundary issues, we can usually trace it back to two things: Their family lacked boundaries or the person experienced the mean girl syndrome in middle school or high school or were mistreated by classmates on a regular basis.

One of the most common forms of boundary violations within families is "getting into each other's business." There is an extreme lack of privacy. If you came from this type of family, you might have experienced some of the following: The Spanish Inquisition was frequent, and you were expect to reveal all the details of a date, party, phone conversation, a play date, etc. The result of sharing a secret or an experience with a single family member was that everyone knew your business, as if it were posted on a bulletin board for all to view. If you grew up in one of these families, meddling is perceived as a way of expressing love, interest and being protective.

In other families, intimacy and talking about feelings was discouraged. If you shared your feelings, you were told to suck it up, were made fun of or were punished in some way (i.e. a child expresses hurt over how a parent disciplined them, and as a result, the parent tacks on further punishment). These responses cause a disconnection in one's ability to set proper boundaries. Not setting boundaries becomes a survival technique to avoid pain. The person stops asking for their needs to be met because they experience pain (emotional or physical) when they make their needs or feelings known.

Secondly, the experiences someone has in high school or middle school can contribute greatly to a person's inability to set proper boundaries. This is the time in your life when you are coming into your own and developing character.

For men, it is the time when the "alpha males" appear in the pack. Men are much more likely to tell another male that they don't like something or tell another male to back off. Sometimes, there is a physical altercation, but more often just strongly making the request to back off is enough and things blow over relatively quickly.

Our son is a good-natured young man. He is pretty easy going, but there were a few occasions in middle school and high school when he was involved heated arguments with other boys. These were not actually fights, but an exchange of sharp words, raised voices, and a bit of physical intimidation like getting in each other's face or causing the other boy to take a step back. Without coming to physical blows, these young men expressed their physical and emotional boundaries and the disagreement was over. However, if our son had backed down, fearing that he might get pummeled in a physical fight, he most likely would have been picked on by the other boys in the future. If you are a male who backs down, chances are that you were bullied in high school or middle school. A man who has been bullied, either emotionally or physically, bullies his partner (because it worked for the people that bullied him) or will continue to get walked on. Neither of these is healthy.

Girls, on the other hand, aren't as forthright about setting boundaries. When a girl gets into a confrontation, instead of being direct and expressing that she feels that her boundaries have been violated, females typically use the covert approach. Instead of talking with the person who hurt or disappointed her, females gather together their posse and begin back stabbing, spreading rumors and shutting the other girl out of the clique. Sound familiar? This is the "mean girl syndrome" which determines who are the most popular girls (who is in and who is out!), at least for that day or week!

This is how it starts: Usually it is a single incident in which you set a boundary by telling your friend that something she said or did hurt you. You talked it through, she says she is sorry and you are back to being friends. However, the next day you show up at school and your entire group of friends is being cruel and hateful towards you. This band of girls is being led by your remorseful friend. You've been hit by the "boundary backfire."

When a female is hit by the "boundary backfire", she learns not to approach someone head-on, but instead, to get together her entourage of supporters before going into battle. And so the "mean girl syndrome" begins. Who can you trust? Who plays the game better than the other? Who can you recruit to your side? While this is the norm for most women, most healthy men consider this behavior to be ridiculous, confusing, female "drama" and will put up with the childish behavior for only a short while.

So, here comes the interesting part. Men and women bring what they have learned about setting boundaries when they attempt to create a healthy relationship. A man comes into a love relationship believing that the woman will tell him if something is wrong but the woman doesn't. The woman believes that the man should "figure it out" by observing her reactions (cold shoulder, being distant, talking with friends and hoping it gets back to him). Many times, men have learned to express their boundaries with strong words and sometimes even a bit of intimidation. Women feel this way of expressing boundaries is oppressive. No matter how you slice it, all of these methods of setting boundaries are immature. This is why learning new ways of setting boundaries is so important! So listen up! Let's walk through the process of setting healthy boundaries.

Principles of Boundaries

You teach people how to treat you! If you don't say anything but something is bothering you, you are telling the person that their behaviors or actions are okay. You get what you tolerate!

What are Boundaries?

One of the keys to successful dating is having clear, healthy boundaries in your dating life and relationships. Simply put, a boundary is the space a person needs physically or emotionally to feel comfortable with another person.

The different types of boundaries as listed below:

- The emotional space between two people.

- The physical space between two people.

- A line which you will not let someone cross because of the negative impact of crossing that line in the past.

- Clear delineation of where you end and the other person begins.

- Your expectation that someone respects your physical and emotional well-being.

- Healthy physical and emotional distance so that you don't become co-dependent.

- Appropriate emotional and physical connection you need to maintain so that you and another person do not become too detached and/or dependent.

- Balance of time, emotional limits and physical limits to achieve an interdependent relationship verses a dependent relationship. By doing so, you maintain your personal identity, uniqueness, and autonomy.

- Physical or emotional limits that are clearly defined so you feel free to be yourself. This means you are able to think, feel or act without restrictions placed on you by others

How are the boundaries in your life? Some people are very aware of their boundaries. Through our coaching practice, we have observed that most people really struggle with setting clear boundaries. There are several reasons people resist setting boundaries:

• Fear of confrontation

• Fear of someone not liking them

• Fear of someone saying "NO"

• Fear of being abandoned

Notice the word FEAR. People who don't set up boundaries are afraid that if they ask for what they need to be comfortable and happy, they won't get their needs met. More importantly, they fear that others will be unhappy. Boundaries are simply requesting that someone honor your physical and emotional space in this great universe of ours. You are responsible for establishing what that means for you. If you establish reasonable boundaries and someone says no, or they are unhappy, show them the door! You don't need to waste your time on people like this!

There are two ways of negotiating boundaries. The first way, and the most common, is passive. Passively negotiating boundaries is very passive-aggressive. You fail to tell someone directly what you need to feel safe in a relationship. Instead, you give them verbal or emotional clues and hope they figure it out. We'll explain these clues later in the chapter.

The second way of getting your needs met is by actively negotiating boundaries. This consists of telling the other person how their actions, behavior or words affected you and requesting they do something different in the future.

Boundaries are a way of actively negotiating a relationship. All relationships are negotiated. They are either negotiated actively or passively. The decision is yours to make. There is a huge benefit to actively negotiating your relationships. What is that benefit? You have a much higher probability of getting what you want and need. But, isn't that what we all really want? If you are actively negotiating relationships, you are letting others know what does and does not work for you in your relationship.

Now, let's take a closer look at passively negotiating a relationship. If you are passively negotiating relationships, you are establishing boundaries by default. When something comes up that you don't like, or perhaps it hurts you emotionally/physically, you let it go. This tells the other person that their actions were okay with you. If their actions weren't okay the first time, then why didn't you tell them?

Here is an example: You are dating someone and they cancel a date with you at the last minute because something came up at work. You tell them it is okay. You have, in fact, told them it is alright to cancel at the last minute. Later, if they cancel a date at the last minute and you get upset, they are going to wonder why. It was previously alright with you when it happened. That is because you passively negotiated. It is that simple. When you don't let people know that something has negatively affected you, you've told them that their actions or hurtful words are okay.

If it isn't alright with you, telling them is simply the best thing. You can calmly and politely say something like, "I am really disappointed. I was looking forward to the evening. I know sometimes things come up but I really would appreciate it if you could call earlier so I can make other plans." You can make a strong direct request in a calm and polite way. You don't have to say it in a harsh angry tone. You will get better results if your tone of voice is not inflammatory.

If it keeps happening, you might want to handle it this way. "I notice that you seem to be canceling our dates when something else comes up. When you do this, it makes me feel like I am not as important and it really bothers me. I need to know that you feel my time is valuable, too." This is an example of setting a boundary.

Early Warning Signs of Unhealthy Boundaries

Earlier in the book, we brought up the subject of being bitten by the "Love Bug." One of the symptoms of the "Love Bug's" bite is throwing aside boundaries. Sometimes we want to be in a relationship so badly that we ignore setting up healthy boundaries for fear of losing the relationship.

It could be that you suffer from boundaries that are unhealthy or unclear. Take a look at the following list. Be honest with yourself. Are you dating someone with unhealthy boundaries or do you have unhealthy boundaries? We are writing this as if it is YOU, but it could be someone you are dating or have been in a relationship with who lacks these boundaries.

- You either trust no one or trust anyone without knowing if someone is trustworthy.

- You share way too much about your life with someone with whom you have little or no personal relationship or connection.

- On a first meeting, you talk at intimate level about feelings, desires, dreams and life goals.

- You easily fall in love with a new acquaintance.

- If someone emotionally reaches out to you, you tend to easily fall in love.

- You become preoccupied or overwhelmed by a person and can't seem to get them out of your mind.

- When you have a sexual impulse, you act on it.

- You have sex with someone because you feel pressured or feel that they will leave you if you don't.

- You dismiss your personal values or rights to please others.

- Being oblivious to personal boundaries, you do not notice when someone else displays inappropriate boundaries or when someone invades your boundaries.

- You accept food, gifts, touch, sex that you don't want.

- You touch a person without asking.

- You take as much as you can get for the sake of getting.

- You give as much as you can give for the sake of giving.

- You allow others to take as much as they can from you.

- You surrender your life decisions over to someone and let them direct your life.

- You let others define your reality, including telling you how you should feel or what you are feeling.

- You believe others can anticipate your needs, and you expect them to automatically fill those needs.

- You emotionally fall apart so someone will take care of you.

- You participate in self-abuse including self-destructive behaviors, addictions, cutting, anorexia, bulimia, and over-eating.

- You either sexually abuse or are sexually abused.

- You either physically abuse or are being physically abused.

When you are bitten by the "Love Bug", a lot of people have the desire to spend every waking moment with their new love interest. We all need time to attend to our lives and other relationships. If you don't set boundaries, you will regret it later. You will not have any time for yourself and you risk losing yourself in the relationship. Have you ever been in a relationship that ended and you realized that you hadn't spent any time with your friends or family in months? Having a balance in your life is important. You need to continue to live your life and incorporate your new relationship into it. You are responsible for directing your own life and defining your reality. You have to know yourself well enough so that you don't lose who you are in a relationship.

A friend of ours has been in several serious relationships. In all of the relationships, the charming, fun-loving man that we know disappears. We refer to him as "the chameleon." He isn't clear about his own personal values and beliefs, so he takes on the values and beliefs of his partner. He totally changes his personality. He is letting someone else define his reality and who he is as a person. As a result, most of his friendships have fallen away.

The rush-rush-hurry-hurry tendency to get into a relationship too quickly can also backfire on you. It can lead you to share too much information about yourself too early in the relationship. The "tell all" spills their guts about everything that has ever happened to them, (mostly the bad stuff), life philosophy and intimate details of past love relationships after knowing someone for a short time.

When a client proclaims that they know someone really well after a few dates, we know they have been doing a "data dump" while on their dates. The relationship looks like it is taking off like a rocket, but usually it runs out of rocket fuel early.

Take your time getting to know someone. You don't have to answer every question someone asks you. One of our favorite ways to respond to a question that we are not comfortable answering is by saying, "That is an interesting question. I'm curious to know why you are asking about that." If you tend to "vomit" information, relax, slow down, and think before you just blurt something out.

Set some boundaries. You don't know a person very well when you first start dating. They are a stranger to you. You don't have to give them your whole life story. Leave some mystery to who you are and what you are all about. You don't have to be an open book. Let them have a peek at the first few chapters of your life and leave them wanting more. Our rule of thumb is: If you wouldn't tell it to the person behind you in the grocery store checkout line, don't spill it on your first few dates. Sharing your vulnerabilities early in the dating process can be risky. You don't know if your new love interest is going to gently hold your heart in their hands or spike it like a football.

Choosing to be closed off to interacting with someone because you don't trust anyone is no better than being a "tell all." You can't develop intimacy if you aren't willing to take a risk. You have to strike a happy medium between the "tell all" and the "tell nothing." Be yourself and let others see the real you.

The person who professes their love after just a few dates has boundary issues. In addition, this person is confusing chemistry with love. Love takes a long time to develop. Someone who wants to rush into the relationship is either emotionally immature or needs to close the deal before you find out their true nature. Either way, it isn't good. You also don't want to be a person who accepts the love of someone just to be in a relationship. You will feel empty inside in the long run. You want to be in a relationship with the right person who meets your needs.

Have you ever been the person who gives, gives, gives in relationships hoping that the other person will eventually give back? But instead, they continue to take. For example: You are home cooking him/her a nice dinner and you call to request that they stop to get some wine on their way home. They respond not with wine, but with a whine. "I'm tired and I don't feel like going to the store." There is no thought about you. It is what works for them and them only. This is the selfish taker.

You also have to check yourself. If you continue to be in a relationship with a taker, and you give and give, you will be taken for granted. People who allow others to take advantage of them and complain about how they are getting used have boundary issues. No one can take advantage of you unless you give them permission by not setting boundaries. Here is the interesting side of it: Most people who feel used also feel needed. Do you have a strong need to feel needed? UMMMM!

Being a taker can feel just as yucky. Sometimes you are with someone who is a giver. They buy you clothes, groceries, a cell phone and lots of other goodies. You accept the gifts because you don't want to hurt their feelings, but in the back of your mind, you know they are trying to buy your love. You often lose respect for the giver, but if they are willing to give, why shouldn't you take? If you want to be in a relationship with someone you can respect, don't accept gifts from someone who you know is trying to buy your love.

Another obstacle that might impede someone's ability to get into a healthy relationship is not letting go of a past relationship before entering into a new one. Some people can never let go of the muck from a previous relationship and, as a result, they talk at length about their past relationship partner. If you continue to listen to their endless babble about their "ex", you won't be able to focus on what is really important; your relationship. This is not a strong foundation to build a healthy relationship upon.

Jeannine's Former Boundary Issues

I now chuckle at one of my former boundary issues but I am sure that it was extremely frustrating for the men I dated. I expected the men in my life to automatically know what made me happy and what made me upset. "If they loved me, they should just know." A person who believes that the other person should anticipate and fulfill their needs has unhealthy boundaries and expectations. (Guilty as charged.) Expecting someone to have ESP will surely be a disaster! You have to be comfortable enough with your partner to discuss each other's boundaries.

Everyone is responsible for their own feelings and their own needs. If someone's needs aren't getting met, it is probably because they aren't asking. Just as it is your responsibility to set boundaries in your life and ask for what you want, your partner must be able to do the same thing. It isn't your job, nor is it their job, to guess!

Have you met a person who falls apart so someone will take care of them and help put them back together? WOW! Super boundary issues here. This is usually a person who has got attention throughout their life by creating a crisis. They repeat the pattern in dating and hope for a white knight/angel to come and rescue them. If you are the white knight/angel, you have boundary issues as well.

Sex can be a stumbling block in setting boundaries. Sometimes a person can initiate sex too early because they believe that sex moves a relationship forward or because they are acting on impulse. Sometimes one partner will want the other person to engage in sexual acts that do not feel comfortable to them. When the pressured person eventually gives in, resentment can grow from being pressured sexually.

We had a client who dated a man who wanted her to do a strip tease for him. She didn't feel comfortable doing it but because he called her a prude, she felt she had to prove something. She went home feeling bad about the experience and ended the relationship the next day. If you allow someone to pressure you into something, you might end up feeling empty and resentful. This is not a good foundation for building a healthy love relationship.

It is also important to identify the signs that your boundaries are being violated. One of the key resources to doing this is your personal feelings. It is that little voice inside your head that tells you something is wrong or doesn't feel right. That little voice is an important guidance system which should not be ignored.

Signs of Violated Boundaries

It is crucial to understand when you are showing symptoms of violated boundaries. If you lack boundaries, you probably won't see these violations while you are in a relationship. Take the time to examine them. If, in the past, you have shown any of the following signs, you need to learn how to set boundaries!

Over-Enmeshment: This is the belief that both people have to do everything together, think alike, feel and act the same way in a relationship. No one is allowed to deviate from the relationship norms. The relationship looks homogeneous. Uniqueness and autonomy are viewed as deviation from the norm.

Disassociation: A key symptom of "disassociation" is blanking out when a very stressful, emotional event occurs. You seem to check out and stop feeling.

- You feel your emotional or physical space being violated, but you tell yourself that it doesn't matter.

- If you ignore it; it will go away.

- No sense in fighting it; it will be over soon.

- Don't fight it. It will make it worse.

Blanking out results in you not being in touch with your feelings about what happened. Sometimes you will not remember what happened. Has this ever happened to you? You might have heard of this happening to someone who experiences some traumatic event, like an auto accident. They don't remember what happened. This is a survival mechanism. It can happen in a relationship when something becomes too stressful. This can also be a sign that you are in an abusive relationship.

Excessive Detachment: This occurs when you are unable to establish any connection of emotions or feelings with another person. One or both people in the relationship are totally independent of each other. There doesn't seem to be anything holding them together. People who fear losing themselves in relationships will detach.

Victim Mode: You identify yourself as a victim and become defensive to ward off future attacks or violations. Another reaction is to self-identify as a victim in the relationship and then to continue to allow behavior that makes you feel victimized, thus letting you be the martyr. The martyr role is learned, usually by watching and identifying with a parent who plays this role in their marriage and in life.

The Chip on the Shoulder: Something has happened that really hurt you. To deal with the hurt, you combine an underlying anger, like a volcano ready to erupt at the most unpredictable time, with a cold, aloofness. It is as if you are daring someone to come too close. Neither of you can predict what will happen if they do come close, but it won't be good.

Invisibility: Your goal is to not be seen or heard so that you don't have to let someone know how you are really feeling. This is also known as withdrawing. You try not to get noticed, to be invisible. If you aren't noticed then you can avoid pain.

Aloofness or Shyness: When you have been ignored or rejected in the past, you might take these stances. Aloofness and shyness are a form of rejecting others. You want to reject others before they reject you.

Cold and Distant: You build up high walls around you to keep people away. If someone doesn't enter your personal space, they can't hurt you.

This is a way to keep others out and put them off. It is usually brought on by previous pain caused from being ignored, hurt or rejected. This is often the "I'll show you" stance. You hurt me, so I will ignore you and see how you feel.

Smothering: This is when you are not allowed to have your own space, either physically or emotionally. The feeling can be overwhelming. A person who feels smothered feels held too tightly and experiences a lack freedom to function on their own.

Lack of Privacy: This is when what you are thinking, feeling or doing is not your own business. You are expected to report all the details and content of your feelings, reactions, opinions, relationships and dealings with others to your partner. You begin to think that nothing is private and there is no place you can escape to be your own person.

If you can identify with one or more of these sign, you have been in a relationship that lacked healthy boundaries. Don't you think it is about time that you to learn to set boundaries in your life and in your relationships?

How Do You Set Healthy Boundaries?

You can know the signs of unhealthy boundaries in dating and relationships, but if you don't know how to set a boundary, you are going to get stuck.

We are going to give you the six steps to setting healthy boundaries. If you apply these principles, you will be able to establish healthy relationships in your life.

STEP 1: Ask for what you want and need. A healthy, loving person will respect your boundaries. If they do not, you need to restate your needs. Let them know that you can't be in a relationship with someone who will not respect your boundaries. You have to mean it. If you set a boundary and it is violated, but then you do or say nothing about the violation, you lose credibility and personal power.

STEP 2: Remember that "NO!" is a complete sentence. If you tell someone "NO!" and they don't respect it, the answer is still "NO!" You don't owe someone an explanation unless you want to give it.

STEP 3: Have trust in yourself. Your partner can have your best interest in mind, but you need to follow your own heart and your feelings. You can't surrender your well-being to someone else. Know what you want and need. If something doesn't feel right, your highest good is not being served. You get to ask for what makes you happy and feel honored by the other person.

STEP 4: If someone hurts you emotionally, you have to let them know how. These are your feelings and you should express them. If someone doesn't honor the fact that you were hurt by their words or actions, they really don't care about you or your heart. Often, the person did not mean to hurt you. However, if they do not recognize or acknowledge your experience and commit to not doing it again, you have a problem.

STEP 5: Be kind, but firm, when you are setting a boundary. Take responsibility for your feelings. No one can make you feel a certain way without your consent. You are responsible for your own feelings. But, you can let your loved one know that they triggered your feelings through their words or actions.

STEP 6: Make a request. Tell the other person how you want to be treated in the future. Remember that you should not expect your partner to figure out your feeling and emotions. Tell them what you need or want!

Setting a boundary might look like this:

When you didn't call me and you said you would, it made me feel worried and upset. I became concerned that something happened to you. It is important to me that you keep your word and commitments to me. When you say you are going to call, please call.

To simplify, here is the formula:

1. State the boundary violation: When you_____ (didn't call me and you said you would)

2. State how you felt: I felt_____ (worried, upset, angry etc.) Notice that you aren't saying: "You made me worried and upset." If you start a sentence with "YOU MADE ME FEEL," the other person will immediately go on the defensive.

3. State how it impacted you: When you didn't call, and you said you would, I wondered if something had happened to you.

4. Make a request! What I am requesting is _____ (that you call me if you say you are going to call.) Tell them what you need them to do in the future.

Notice that in the above boundary, the person is clear about the action that triggered the feelings. He/she is clear about how it made them feel. They are also clear about why it is important to them. Lastly, they make a request: "When you say you are going to call, please call." By using this method of communication, the other person is less likely to become defensive.

People who set healthy boundaries early in a relationship will not get abused. A potential abuser will exit the relationship because they need to have complete control. If a person expresses their personal power by setting and maintaining boundaries, they will take away a potential abuser's prime motivation for abusing--control. If someone hurts you physically, there is no excuse to stay in the relationship. Leave! If someone uses their physical presence to intimidate you, leave! At this point, it is not a boundary issue, this is **abuse** and your safety is as stake.

The bottom line is that you have to have self-respect and a positive self-esteem to set healthy boundaries. You have to know that you are worth it. When you lack self-esteem or self-worth, you are more likely to have people walk all over you like a doormat. You weren't born to be a doormat. Becoming a doormat is a choice.

Become clear about your needs. If something doesn't feel good, examine why! Your feelings are your feelings. Discussing how an experience between you and your partner made you feel will help your relationship develop a new wonderful level of intimacy. Don't be afraid that someone will leave you if you express yourself. If they leave, they were definitely not the right partner for you.

Here are some questions to ask yourself to determine if you have established healthy boundaries:

- Is this relationship in my best interest?

- Are my needs being met?

- Are his/her needs being met?

- Are we getting to know each other at a comfortable pace?

- Am I spending too much time and energy trying to make sense out of this person's actions?

- Is this person keeping the agreements we make?

- Does this person seem to want a reciprocal relationship?

It is important to be able to set healthy boundaries to develop a well-balanced loving relationship. Without boundaries, we are doomed to lose our self and our needs in relationships and grow to resent our partners. We are responsible for what we get in our relationships. We train people how to treat us.

CHAPTER 11

Cupid Simplifies the Dating Game

You are reading this book because you want to find your ideal mate. We are so excited for you. It is so wonderful when you find the person who complements you and your life. The process of finding your ideal mate can be just as enjoyable.

Why do people date? Most of you would answer this question by saying, "To get married, of course." That might be the end result that many people are seeking. However, there are people out there who are dating just to have fun. (Jeannine and Keith were in that mode for a while until they met.) There are others who are just looking for a sexual relationship. There is nothing wrong with either of these goals. In fact, many of the people who just want to have fun learn more about their dates than the people who are looking for a relationship. Why? They really don't have anything to lose.

There is something to learn from the people who are not seeking a relationship. Many are having fun meeting new and interesting people. They are going out and doing interesting fun things. If they stop having fun or they don't find the person interesting, they stop dating the person. What a concept!

For a person who is seeking their ideal mate, dating is a process of getting to know someone to determine if you might want to explore a love relationship.

There are three stages of dating and relationships. Understanding these stages will help you make good dating choices and help you recognize when you have entered into a relationship.

If you are lucky enough to have chemistry with someone, you might experience the *Honeymoon Stage* of a "potential relationship." The *Honeymoon Stage* presents itself with all the craziness of falling in love. Your heart is fluttering, the sky is bluer, the grass greener. The person you are dating seems like the perfect match for you. Both of you are on your best behavior. Hormones are going crazy and you feel like you are on Cloud Nine. This isn't love, but it is definitely CHEMISTRY! Many people get love and chemistry confused. Love takes time to develop and chemistry is almost instantaneous. Often, this is the time where people have sex because they believe they are in love. The *Honeymoon Stage* usually last from one to six months.

Once the fog has cleared from your mind, you might start to realize that you and your potential partner have some differences that need to be addressed. It might be that their actions are making you feel uncomfortable or unappreciated.

Let's say that your date shows up late to pick you up for each date. Or you go to pick them up and they aren't ready. You have to wait around until they finish putting on their makeup and you are late arriving at the play, party or event because they took too long in the bathroom!

Another example might be that your dating partner was rude to one of your friends. They openly criticized the clothes they were wearing causing your friend to be hurt and embarrassed. You were enraged by the comments and you begin to question his/her behavior and lack of tact.

These are signs that you are entering the *Negotiating Stage* of the relationship. You realize that your potential partner isn't perfect. It is time to talk about how their behavior affected you (setting healthy boundaries). If you don't speak up about what they are doing, you are not going to get your needs met in the relationship.

The *Negotiating Stage* of dating and/or a relationship can be marked by the chemistry beginning to wane a bit. There is more emphasis placed on finding out your level of compatibility as a couple. During this phase of dating/relationship, most people are beginning to let their hair down. Often you start seeing the other person's faults, how they do things differently than you, and behaviors that might concern you. You begin to negotiate with your potential partner. You probably will point out things that bother you or make you uncomfortable and request that they don't do those things in the future.

This stage of the relationship is usually riddled with small tiffs and some big disagreements. The outcome depends on how emotionally mature each partner is, and how skilled you are at setting healthy boundaries.

It is important not to get into the position of placing blame on the other person during this stage of the game. Instead, focus on letting your potential partner know that something made you uncomfortable and make requests of what you would prefer instead.

Your ultimate goal during this part of the development of the relationship is to see if you can find common ground. It is not to see who can WIN a disagreement. It isn't about who is RIGHT.

You have to avoid being a "right fighter." The definition of a "right fighter" is the person who has to make the other person wrong in order to be right!

Here is an example of "right fighting":

A man invites a woman over for dinner. When she arrives, she sees the raw chicken and salad ingredients on the kitchen counter. He

pours her a glass of wine and then asks her if she can make the
salad while he puts the chicken on the barbeque. She becomes
furious. He asked her over for dinner and expects her to cook.
After all, when she invites him for dinner, she does all the work.
Because the woman has an opinion of the "right way" to entertain,
she thinks any other way of entertaining is "wrong." What could
have been a nice dinner deteriorates into an argument as their
expectations collide.

The man simply saw this as an opportunity to cook together while
she saw it as inconsideration and a lack of effort. Because she wanted
to make him "wrong" for how he approached preparing the dinner, the
evening was ruined.

In many dating relationships, this over-reaction might be enough to
end the relationship. The *Negotiating Stage* of the relationship is where
most relationships crumble. Couples begin seeing their differences and
lack the skills or desire to negotiate through the process to move to the
relationship forward. The *Negotiating Stage* will last three to twelve
months.

Some people just don't want to change. They want their partner to
meet them exactly where they stand in life. They are set in their ways
and want their partner to accept this. If their partner isn't willing to
change, then they exit the relationship.

Then, there are the people who are addicted to the feeling of "falling
in love" and often leave a relationship during the *Negotiating Stage* to
find their next "falling in love" high. The *Negotiation Stage* feels like
too much work. They just want that excited feeling. If the "relationship
high" begins to dwindle, they move to the next relationship. This is
a lonely endless cycle. You can't get into a true, healthy relationship
without passing through the *Negotiation Stage*.

Once you have successfully established boundaries and negotiated
some of the potential pitfalls or challenges in the relationship, you

are ready to move on. If you can find common ground and come to agreement on some significant and insignificant things, you might be ready for more. This is where couples enter the *Commitment Stage* of the relationship.

Typically, during the *Commitment Stage* the chemistry begins to increase again as a couple realizes that they have a level of commonality and compatibility that could sustain a relationship. Many couples begin planning for their future together. You might begin talking about moving in together or about getting engaged.

There is a level of excitement that comes with this phase of the relationship. (Notice that we didn't say "dating." This is now a relationship.) There is more negotiation as two lives begin to merge together. But there is excitement with this negotiation as you see the possibility of being together, maybe even forever.

This is where we raise the caution flag. Sometimes people stop negotiating the relationship because they are so excited about the possibility of getting married and don't want to rock the boat, at least until there is a ring on your/her finger. No! No! No! This is the time to talk about children, money, where you are going to live and all the other details of blending your lives together.

In healthy relationships and marriages you must have an on-going series of negotiations and it is important to have healthy negotiation skills. You will forever be changing and growing because life is forever changing around you. You might have children, develop financial problems, suffer a job loss, transferred to a new city and all the other things life can throw at you. Life will happen. If you struggled through the *Negotiating Stage,* marriage might be difficult. To move forward, you will need to negotiate and align with the current situation and find a solution that meets both partners' needs. The *Commitment Stage* last, on average, six months-death do you part.

Be willing to say, "Next!" If a relationship isn't moving forward or isn't giving you what you desire, you owe it to yourself to move on. You can't steal second base keeping your foot on first base. Give yourself permission to move on if the person you are dating isn't the right one for you.

The greatest obstacle to finding a great relationship is settling for a good relationship. Sometimes people find themselves in a relationship with a "good" person. Things are okay but they aren't great. In fear of moving on and not finding one better, they stay in the relationship even though it isn't right for them.

Are you willing to get your foot off first base to steal second? Isn't your goal to find the right relationship? Well, don't waste time in a relationship or dating situation that doesn't give you that possibility. The quicker you move on, the quicker you can find someone who is your match. When you stay with someone who is not your match, you are not only are robbing yourself of the potential to find your ideal mate, but you are robbing your partner of that possibility, too.

If you don't have a match on values and long-term goals; marriage, having children, traveling, spiritual growth, planning for your future, common activities, and chemistry, then you need to move on. You want the right match, not just someone to marry. Marriage can be a very lonely place if you aren't in the right relationship. It is easy to grow apart and become a divorce statistic if you don't have a solid base for the relationship.

CHAPTER 12

Sex and Being Single

You might not be a prude when it comes to having sex. You moved to the experienced category when you could no longer count your lovers on your fingers and toes. Or, maybe you hang onto your virginity tighter than a toddler hugs a security blanket. Your virginity is a sign that you are one of the "good girls." You use your virginity to ward off sexual advances by saying, "I will only have sex after I am married." (This can go for men, too.)

If you are re-entering the dating world after divorce and in the past you warded off sexual advances by holding up the virginity shield, you might have to change your strategy. If you are re-entering the dating world as a divorcee and mother of three children, rebuffing sex by claiming you are a virgin is a thing of the past. You aren't going to fool anyone.

Most people we speak with about sex say that they should not have slept with most of their lovers. Half of them weren't that good in bed. And those who pressured them into having sex dropped off their radar screen shortly after their romp between the sheets.

We get asked advice about sex all the time, mostly from women who feel the pressure to have sex with men so they'll stick around. Sorry girls, that doesn't work. We've seen it in action. If a man is going to stick around, it is because he is really into you as a person.

It seems that singles are having sex earlier and earlier in the dating process. It isn't unheard of to have sex on the first or second date. In fact, it is pretty darn common. It seems like women are willing to have sex earlier and earlier and men are expecting it. Women are creating a culture of casual sex that they really don't want. Every woman who is having sex early in the dating process is doing a disservice not only to herself, but to all the other women who will date the man later.

One thing hasn't changed: Men will say just about anything to get a woman to have sex. Is there a secret club out there that teaches men what to say to get women in bed? So many men have the same lines, but women don't seem to notice. They flatter you and make you feel like they have never met anyone like you. They can't wait to spend more time with you. Bait, hook and reel them in. Women fall for this hook, line and sinker.

Sex can really complicate the development of a relationship. Once a couple moves to sexual intimacy, there is a shift in the emotional development. There are very few women who don't start thinking about where the relationship is going after engaging in "the wild thing."

Often, their expectations of the man changes; they expect him to act more like a committed partner. Sex does not mean that a couple is in a committed relationship, but many women believe that sex implies a commitment. This is where things start to get confusing and messed up.

When a relationship is new, the couple is excited about each other. Chemistry can lead people to believe that there is more to the potential relationship than will be uncovered with time. They have sex and feel this transforms them into "boyfriend and girlfriend." Then they start to get to know each other better and find out that there really isn't a good match. Having sex makes it more difficult to end the dating relationship than if they had never engaged in sex and were simply dating.

Getting dumped shortly after "putting out" never feels good. It can make you feel used, or worse, like a disappointment in bed. Either way, it is going to impact your self-esteem. Don't think for a moment that this doesn't happen to men, too. Women can use men to scratch that itch and then turn around and dump them.

If you are serious about finding a long-lasting partnership, then you will want to wait until a foundation is in place before you jump into bed together. Potentially solid partnerships with two good people often get destroyed because they had sex too early, before they really got to know each other.

Ideally, you want to make sure you both agree that you are in a monogamous committed relationship before having sex. A general rule of thumb is to not have sex with someone before you can and do comfortably talk about sex with them.

Some people strongly disagree with this philosophy because they believe that talking about sex before hand will kill the spontaneity. But, the spontaneity can still be there. You can have an even deeper connection, because you won't be as distracted with all of your worries or thoughts about their thoughts as you share those first intimate moments together.

You should be able to talk about what hasn't worked for you in the past in your sexual relationships, measures you take for birth control and protection against disease. You should be able to discuss what would happen if a pregnancy occurred; what would you do?

If you aren't ready to have sex and your partner is pressuring you, he or she might not be the right partner. Honoring your feelings is an important part of any long-term healthy relationship.

CHAPTER 13

Dating with a Purpose

For now, we want you to focus on getting clear about you want. In Steven Covey's book, *The 7 Habits of Highly Effective People*, Covey encourages people to start with the end in mind. We are encouraging you to do just that. What do you want as the end result of dating and exploring a relationship? We are going to teach you to become an effective dater.

To become an effective dater, you must enter the dating world with a single goal; to become crystal clear about the type of person with whom you want to marry or have a committed long-term relationship. Dating isn't just the process of finding your mate. The dating process can be a fun way of learning what you want in a mate. If you approach dating with this intention the dating process can be fun, exciting and productive. Not every date is going to be a love match. However, there is something to learn from every person you date. The things you will learn will lead you closer and closer to your ideal mate.

What is dating? It is much more that the process of finding Mr. or Ms. Right. In dating, you are defining who you are, what you want in a relationship and screening potential applicants. Dating is a unique opportunity to learn more about you, meet new people, network, and have positive impacts on other human beings. When handled well, dating can be the start to a wonderful romantic relationship and it can expand one's personal network of friends. You might meet someone who isn't right for you but they may have a friend that would be a perfect match for you.

We've probably heard life's Golden Rule, "*Treat others as you would like to be treated.*" In dating and relationships this rule requires a slight modification to be truly effective. At our Soul Mate Quest seminars we teach the Soul Mate Quest Rule which is to "*Treat others as they would like to be treated;*" realizing that what we like is not necessarily what our partner will like. We must also understand that others many not always reciprocate in kind. If you are kind, even when you don't have a love match, you are living by a higher standard.

Don't give someone hope that you will go out with them again just to spare yourself a little discomfort. And there is no reason to be cowardly, mean or cruel when ending a dating relationship. When dating is not handled well, it can leave the other person feeling rejected, hurt and confused. You can kindly let some know that you don't have a love match but wish them luck in finding "the one."

Every date can and should be a learning opportunity. You might meet some amazing men/women and many of them will have wonderful qualities that you appreciate but they might not be a love match. Extrapolate the qualities that you like in these men/women and add these qualities to your ideal relationship list.

Sometimes a date won't even be a close match. Translating the traits, behaviors, goals, values and communication styles of these people that you did not like can help you to better understand what you do want. You should ask yourself several questions after each date.

- What did I learn about myself from this date?

- Did I see any qualities that I desire in my ideal mate?

- Was there something that I didn't like and if so, what do I want instead?

EXERCISE: Keep A Dating Journal

Keep a dating journal. Answer the above questions after every date. This will help you create your ideal mate list. Each date gives you an opportunity to discover what you want in your life partner. Write it down or it might be forgotten.

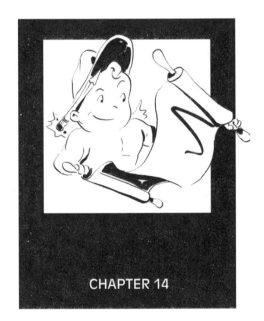

CHAPTER 14

Making Your Relationship List

First of all, let's define a relationship list. A relationship list is simply a written list of the qualities in a partner that you desire and would make you happy. Both of us had lengthy lists; Jeannine's list was actually seven hand-written pages long and Keith's list was three typed pages. Both of us got almost everything we desired when we found each other. Most people don't get everything they want. You are going to have to make some concessions. Nobody is perfect.

Writing your list down on paper is very powerful. If you don't have your list on paper, you really don't have a list. If you are like most singles, you might tell us that you have your list in your head. You cannot have a clear list in your head because a true relationship list can be quite lengthy.

If your list is short and all you require is that they are breathing and have all their teeth, you are being a wimpy-wanter. You deserve to have a wonderful mate. Take the time to write down your list. You'll be glad you did.

Why is a relationship list important? If you aren't clear about what you want, how will you know if you have met the right person? He or she might be right under your nose.

Recently, we had lunch with a lovely woman. She is thirty years old and really wanted to find her ideal mate. She is beautiful, articulate and successful. She had all the qualities that make her a great catch. We were surprised to learn that she had never been in a long-term relationship. Being the inquisitive coaches we are, we asked her what she wants in her ideal mate. She struggled to give us a list. Finally she said, "I guess I don't really know." We recommended that she make a list of all the qualities that would make someone an ideal mate. She balked at our suggestion of creating a relationship list.

This woman gave us the perfect opportunity to prove our point about making the relationship list. We had just driven to the restaurant in her brand new Mercedes. She was very excited about her new car. We took the opportunity to ask her how she decided on buying the Mercedes. She told us that it was her dream car. She had picked out the color, the interior and all the wonderful "bells and whistles", which she listed with expertise. We pointed out that she had put more thought into picking out her car than her future man. We saw a light go on. The next time we saw her, she had started her relationship list.

Making a lifetime commitment to a future mate is a wonderful but challenging decision. It is one of the biggest decisions you will make in your life. Take the time to make the right decision. Start a relationship list today. Take some time to think about your past relationships and how they influenced who you are and how you think today.

When we coach someone who is on the quest to find their ideal mate, we ask them to list what they want. Most people begin their list by saying, "They have to be loving, kind, caring, fun..." Then the list begins to trail off into the "don't wants." I don't want him to have addictions of any kind. I don't want him to be a workaholic. On and on they go.

Refocusing your thoughts and energies into what you want is so important. You will learn more about this in the chapter, "Becoming an

Attraction Magnet." For now, we want you to spend some quality time getting clear about what you want.

As you begin the amazing process of getting clear about your ideal mate, we want you to get really excited. Remember that anticipation when you were a child on Christmas morning and the excitement you felt seeing all the presents spread out under the Christmas tree? Do you remember how you couldn't wait to see what was in each and every package as you ripped off the bows and paper? Or when you had a birthday party and you finished eating cake and it was time to open your birthday presents. Do you remember how eager and excited you became? That is how we want you to feel about this process. Getting excited will help you become more positive and help you focus on what you want.

The clearer and more excited you become about your ideal mate, the faster he/she will come into your life. To help you become clear, we are going to introduce you to a great tool. It is a tool we call **The Clarity Bridge.** This tool helps you to use the things you don't desire to get clear about the things you do.

What you don't desire in a relationship is simply the contrast to the things you do desire. You might not know what you want because you haven't experienced it yet, but examining the things you don't want can help you begin to examine your desires. In order to do this, you need to ponder the question, "If I don't want this or that quality, then what do I want instead?"

Draw your inspiration from all your dating experiences and past relationships. Observe the relationship between your parents. Take a look at the relationships of your siblings and friends. Anything you observe can become part of your relationship list, whether in the "Don't Wants" or "Desires" category. Be honest. No one needs to see your list.

The Clarity Bridge looks a lot like the old Ben Franklin method of making decisions. You've probably seen the trusty pros and cons list. It is set up the same way, but it functions very differently. Draw a line down the center of a page of paper. Put another line across the top of the page horizontally. List your "Don't Wants" on the right side of the paper. You will be listing your "Desires" or "Do Wants" on the left side of the paper. On the line at the top of your page, write **My Ideal Mate.**

Start with your "*Don't Wants*". You already know what you don't want. Whatever you have observed or experienced in love relationships that did not work for you goes on the "*Don't Wants*" side of the paper (right). Don't move to your "*Do Wants*" until you have a complete list of "don't wants"

It is very important that you follow these directions. The reason you will list all of your "*Don't Wants*" first is that one "*Don't Want*" will jog your mind into remembering another "*Don't Want*". You will get into the flow of it. The same goes for what you desire. You will write down something you want and it will give birth to another desire. Don't break the flow. Go with how your mind works.

We read from left to right. The reason for writing your "*Desires*" on the left and "*Don't Wants*" on the right is we are going to get rid of the "*Don't Wants*". You focus only on your desires when this exercise is over.

Have a good time with this but don't be afraid to look in all the dark corners. We have created a list of areas to explore. Feel free to add your own. After all, this is your ideal mate, not ours.

Areas to explore:

- Communication
- Relationships with Family and Friends
- Physical Attraction
- Health/Fitness
- Money
- Sex
- Religion/Spirituality
- Finances/Money
- Career
- Self-Worth
- Emotional Availability
- Values
- Life Dreams and Goal
- Children
- Common Interests
- How You Spend Time (together and apart)
- Being in Partnership in Life
- Travel
- Emotional Health
- Things You'd Like to Try

The Clarity Bridge Example

What I Desire	What I Don't Want
Communicates, listens and is honestly in touch with their feelings. Honors my feelings and opinions. Really listens to what I need and believes that my needs are important. Encourages me to open up more and express how I feel. Really wants to understand my needs, feelings and opinions.	*Doesn't know how to communicate, talk openly and honestly or listen. Dismisses my feelings and opinions.*

What I Desire	What I Don't Want
Has dealt with family relationships and set healthy boundaries. Makes our relation-ship the most important thing in his life, and his family and friends understand and respect this because of his clarity. Has a healthy balance of time with me, friends and family. Really enjoys our time together and makes me a top priority, but also has good friends and likes to spend time with them.	*Doesn't have good relationships with family and friends. Doesn't know how to set healthy boundaries. Doesn't have many friends and relies too much on me.*

What I Desire	*What I Don't Want*
Takes pride in their appearance and well-being by keeping fit through exercise and healthy eating habits. Consistent but not excessive grooming and regular medical and dental check-ups. Overall their grooming reflects a feeling of personal respect and care.	*Doesn't take good care of his body and is out of shape. Isn't well-groomed.*

What I Desire	*What I Don't Want*
Believes in planning for the future but also living for today. They are a great money manager and actively involved in planning for retirement. Can be generous when the occasion calls for it and wants to please me when selecting a gift for my birthday, holiday or an anniversary by selecting thoughtful gifts. Although they are talented in making financial decisions they value my input and we are excited making decisions together regarding investments and major financial purchases.	*Has poor money management skills and hasn't planned for retirement. Is capable of working but isn't. Is overly concerned about money and therefore extremely frugal. Looking for someone to support them. Believes the man should make all the financial decisions in the family.*

What I Desire	What I Don't Want
My partner is a gentle loving sexual partner who enjoys exploring new things in bed and wants to please me. He/She spends time to arouse me so we both reach a wonderful sexual climax. My partner understands when I've had a hard day at work or with the children and just cuddles with me and makes me feel loved.	*Is sexually inexperienced or selfish. Not willing to explore new things in bed or engage in foreplay to enhance our sexual pleasure. Is rough during sex.*

What I Desire	What I Don't Want
They are religious or spiritual with an open mind towards my beliefs and will go to church with me on special occasions, or perhaps, more. Likes to pray together. Is curious about my belief in a "higher power" and accepts this as part of who I am.	*Doesn't honor my faith or my need and desire to go to church. Discourages me from my belief in God and following my religion. Never wants to go to church with me.*

What I Desire	What I Don't Want
Likes their work and the people they work with. When talking about their work environment they want my opinion and support, but are willing to take the necessary action to get their needs met at work.	*Doesn't like their work. Complains endlessly about the people or situation at work, but never does anything to change it.*

What I Desire	*What I Don't Want*
My new love is happy with their life accomplishments and who they are as a person. They exude a quiet confidence and feel proud of friends, family, and me for our successes.	*Uses self-deprivation and self-sabotaging behavior such as addictions to avoid taking responsibility for their life. Finds fault in others to feel better about himself/herself and continually puts people down. Is jealous of other people's successes.*

EXERCISE: Your Ideal Mate

Using the above example, create your own Ideal Mate list. Having helped hundreds of people develop their list, we have never seen two lists that were the same. Your ideal mate list will be unique to you and your desires.

Notice that the "Do Want" part of the list above evokes a level of emotion. You should be able to feel what it is like to experience the emotions associated with what you desire. Notice how clear the writer is about what they desire. You need to get super clear.

Some of the most common things we see on relationship lists are things like honesty, integrity, generosity and sense of humor. If you add these things to your list, you need to define what they mean to you.

When defining humor, one person might enjoy a quick wit. Another person might love someone with a dry sense of humor. Another might like someone who can find something funny about small, insignificant things, or can laugh at himself/herself.

Honesty to one person could mean someone who never cheats on their taxes and would go back to the grocery store if a clerk forgets to charge him/her for an item. For someone else, honesty might mean their partner telling him/her the hard truth and being brutally honest about everything. Be careful what you ask for because you might get it. While brutal honesty might work for some people, when you ask your mate if your ass looks big in an outfit, you may want him to say, "No, honey, you look great!" Not "Well, honey, your ass looks big in all your outfits."

We often get asked the question about physical traits being listed on an ideal mate list. We are attracted to people for all different reasons. You can simply put down that you need to be very physically attracted to the ideal person. That is what we did. However, if there are specific physical traits that are highly desirable or repulsive to you, put them on your list.

We've worked with both men and women who were so focused on the physical traits of a potential partner, that they were blinded by lust. They would be involved with a person for months before they realized that they were not at all compatible with them.

We have also met people who were blinded by someone's lifestyle. A few years ago, we observed a relationship between a beautiful woman who fell for a man who was quite wealthy. Her desire to be married to an affluent man blinded her to how poorly he treated her. After years of dating, she wanted a commitment. He gave her a list of things she would have to agree to if he was going to marry her, including a prenuptial agreement. Basically, she was signing herself into a life of servitude to him. She agreed. They were married and then divorced five years later--and she was out on the street with two small children.

Don't be blinded by desires that feed your ego or fantasy lifestyle. If you find someone who is gorgeous or has lots of money and they are very compatible with you and your life, go for it. But don't make looks and money a prerequisite to examining the possibility of a solid relationship with someone.

As we said before, our relationship lists were quite lengthy. Your list might be even longer. It might be shorter. That's okay. It just has to be right for you. Don't be a "Wimpy Wanter." If your standards are low you are going to shortchange yourself. If you feel you are not deserving of a quality human being as a partner, you will attract unsavory people into your experience.

Then, there are those people who want the sun, moon and stars. They want Jupiter and Mars thrown in for good measure. They can't understand why they can never find someone. No one seems to measure up to their high standards. If you are one of these people, you might need to find a different yardstick.

We met a woman who decided that she wanted to be married. She was in her early fifties and had never been married. She never had the desire to be married before. This woman was beautiful and very fit, however she looked older than her age.

We began to explore what she desired in an ideal mate. As we began to search men's profiles online, we discovered something interesting. When we brought up several pictures of different men, we never got past the picture. Her expectations were way out of whack. She wanted a man who looked like a Greek God with a very full head of hair, blue or green eyes, and perfect teeth. She wouldn't even talk about the personality traits she desired until she found the kind of man with all the physical characteristics she desired. She stated that she wanted a man who was so good looking that it would make her friends envious.

Needless to say, we did not take this woman on as a client. We work with people who want to find their ideal mate and that must include the soul connection. She had set up an impossible standard for finding a mate just to feed her ego. We would be willing to place a large bet that she is still single at sixty or choosing unfulfilling relationships.

Are we telling you to compromise? No! We are saying that if you are chasing a person to feed your ego, you might miss your perfect match. You should be attracted to your ideal mate. But the physical characteristics are just a very small part of the package.

Take a look at why you want the traits that are on your ideal mate list. Did you have an experience with a romantic partner that led you add something on your list to protect you from getting disappointed?

We were working with an adorable thirty-six year old who really wanted to get married and have children. She had a beautiful face, a cute figure, and was successful in her career. When we first met this woman, she seemed to have an inflated sense of herself. She stated several times that she was such an amazing catch that men should be chasing her. However, no man ever measured up to this woman's high standards. She had a very narrow scope of what was acceptable in her ideal mate. With each failed relationship, she would up her standards.

She told us that she would not date any man who didn't live within 15 miles of her home. She once had dated a man who lived 30 miles away. When the relationship got to the point of getting really serious, he wasn't willing to move. She developed the belief that a man should live very close to her to prevent this from happening again. Therefore, she wouldn't even consider dating someone who lived more than 15 miles from her home. Whoa! Talk about narrowing the scope. She had set up her own Mission Impossible.

So what was really going on with this young woman? In actuality, she didn't have a good self-esteem. Her *Itty Bitty Shitty Committee* was working over–time. Her biggest flaw was her tendency to be an over-achiever, which lead to a tremendous fear of failing. Her high standards were her way of protecting herself from failing in a relationship.

This young woman's relationship pattern was that she jumped into a relationship quickly, sure that the man was her soul mate. Even though she told us that men should be chasing her, she was the one who would shower the man with her love and attention. In a short time, she would withdraw from the relationship and begin finding fault in her partner. Her partner never knew what hit him. Before long, he either exited the relationship because of her impossible expectations or she dumped him at the curb. Either way, she could say that the person didn't measure up. She was so afraid of failing that she became a "commitment phobic."

To be successful in the process of finding your ideal mate, you have to avoid sabotaging yourself. Don't be like the woman in this story and leave yourself out in the cold. You could miss your ideal mate because you lack flexibility.

The 80/20 Rule in Dating

You probably won't get 100% of what is on your relationship list, but you should be shooting for about 80%. So be sure to identify the most important items on your list. Find ten things that your ideal mate must have. Those are areas that you won't be willing to compromise.

You can only choose ten so choose carefully. You will be using this as another screening tool. When you are dating, you will check the person's compatibility with your *Relationship List*. If a person does not have your top ten qualities you owe it to yourself to move on.

For instance, let's say that your religion is very important to you. You want a partner that shares your faith and is supportive of bringing up children in that faith. This might be an area that you are not willing to compromise. Just be aware that you are limiting the field to those with your religious beliefs. Are you willing to accept a partner who may not be involved in your church but is willing to raise the children your that faith?

If you have strong political opinions, is it important to have your partner share your opinions? Let say that you are a middle of the road Democrat and your boyfriend/girlfriend is a middle of the road

Republican. On Election Day, you can simply joke about going to the polls and canceling out each other's vote. You can have very different opinions on some political hot buttons but still give each other the room to have a different opinion.

You don't want to eliminate a great partner by having unrealistic expectations, but you do want to have a great match. If it is important to you, honor your request. Don't settle for less. There is a big difference between what you must have and what would be ideal.

What might be ideal is that your mate doesn't leave his socks on the floor and piles of magazines in his office. It might be ideal for your mate if you would put the cordless phones on the receiver and close the cabinet doors in the kitchen and bathroom. None of these are deal killers. Alas, some couples make these small, insignificant things deal killers. Often this is because they believe their partner's actions, or lack of action, is saying, "I don't love you!" or "I don't care enough about you to do what you ask." Catch our drift? *Don't sweat the small stuff!*

We were reflecting about the time we watched an episode from the first season of Dr. Phil. A woman was expressing that she didn't feel loved by her husband because she had to remind him to take out the trash. She expressed her frustration that he didn't "care enough about her" to take the trash out without being asked. Dr. Phil agreed and then told the man his wife defined love by his actions. By not taking out the trash, he was sending the message that he didn't love her.

We understood where this woman was coming from but were torn about supporting her position. We often get into a power struggle in relationships when we believe some small, incidental action or lack of action indicates their level of commitment and love.

Who cares when he takes out the trash? Who cares if you have to gently remind him? YOU DO! Is it really worth all that energy though? It takes you five seconds to hang up a phone on the right receiver, but you don't. Does that mean you don't love your mate? It takes five seconds for him to drop his socks in the hamper instead of on the floor. Does it mean he doesn't love you? We think not!

We want you to fast forward a few years and think about yourself as an eighty year old woman or man. You are sitting in your rocking chair on the porch with your ideal mate sitting next to you, holding your hand and smiling lovingly each other. What is important? Is it important that they have a full head of hair? Is it important that they are a few pounds overweight? Think about this very carefully. Life marches on. Time marches on. Gravity exists. What is really important to you?

EXERCISE: Identifying Your Top Ten List

Before reading any further create your Top Ten List and keep it with you. You also can give this Top Ten List to your friends and family when they ask you what you are looking for in a partner. They will have a clearer picture of what you want. If they know someone with the traits you are looking for, they can set you up on a date with a good candidate. Conversely, you may be spared from disastrous blind dates with well-intentioned mismatches.

The exercises in this chapter are very important. Take your time in making the list. Remember that your list is not written in concrete. If you discover that you desire something else, change your list. This list will help you find the right partner.

CHAPTER 15

The Winning Formula

You + Your Ideal Mate = Your Ideal Relationship

Now that you have identified your ideal mate, we are going to help you create your ideal relationship. The clearer you can become about your mate and ideal relationship, the faster he/she will come into your life.

What is an ideal relationship?

- The relationship works for both parties involved.

- ALL healthy relationships are reciprocal. In an ideal relationship, you desire to give to the other person without keeping score and your partner shares the same desire.

- You have commonality in most aspects of life combined with chemistry.

- You both honor each other's view of life, qualities, interests, beliefs and emotions.

- Both people are emotionally healthy and can make the small adjustments necessary to create a relationship together.

- Both parties want to make the other person feel loved, cared for, and honored within the relationship.

- Both parties are willing and able to be in a committed, monogamous relationship.

Creating Your Vision of Your Ideal Relationship

Why is it important to have a clear vision of your ideal relationship? One of the most significant steps in finding your ideal relationship is determining what that relationship looks like. You must be able to develop and hold a clear vision of your ideal relationship and relationship partner during the dating process. This vision becomes the fundamental tool for screening potential partners. If the person you are dating is not a match, you have an obligation to yourself and to the other person to move on. Many people waste years of their life in relationships that don't have the potential to lead to long term relationships.

EXERCISE: Relationship Clarity

For this exercise, pretend that an entire year has passed since you met your ideal mate. Write a letter to a friend or family member describing how your life has changed since the person of your dreams walked into your life. How do you spend your time with your new love? How does he/she treat you? What feelings does the relationship evoke?

Your letter might look like this:

Wow, Jeannine and Keith: Can you believe that entire year has gone by since I met my soul mate? I can't believe how happy I am! I have never been so happy in my life. Meeting my loving partner and sharing this wonderful, loving relationship is a dream come true for me. It's been such an amazing year. Having my partner come home and embrace me at the end of the day with a hug and kiss is so fulfilling. I can't wait to come home from work and be with him.

We have candlelight dinners together. I cook and he cleans up. We talk about our day and our plans for future events. On the weekends, we love to have people over. We both enjoy each other's friends and families. He is great at the BBQ grill and we make the perfect couple when entertaining.

We have the perfect home with an amazing dining room table, perfect to entertain our large extended family and huge group of friends. Our house is very homey and warm. It is filled with our love. We have light music playing in the background and we dance together. We both love dancing and we are even taking ballroom dancing lessons together. You should see us on the dance floor dancing cheek-to-cheek!

Our love life is absolutely wonderful. He is always tender and loving when we make love. We take showers together. For the first time in my life, I feel like the most beautiful woman on the face of the earth. The way he looks at me takes my breath away. I love touching him, caressing him, honoring him and his body, every part of it. He is so delicious. I know he feels the same. I can feel it when I am in his arms. I feel like crying right now writing this, not with tears of sadness, but tears of joy because I can't believe this has happened to ME. Baby, dreams do come true!!!

He is so gentle and warm. There are mornings that I don't want to get out of bed in the morning because he makes me feel so elated and filled. We are a union. He doesn't want to leave me, either. Sometimes, we just lie in bed and talk for hours. We never seem to run out of things to talk about. Sometimes he reads to me in bed and sometimes shares a story as I lie with my head on his shoulder.

He loves to hear me sing. When I am in the kitchen cooking, I often break into song and he sits there listening to me. He tells me how beautifully I sing and that he could listen to me for hours.

He is so amazingly thoughtful. He always calls me during the day. He buys me flowers. He treats me like I'm the most special person in his life. We treasure our friendship and love.

We pray together and go to church on Sunday. He sits next to me and holds my hand while we worship God. We love going away on romantic adventures. We love walking on the beach in the sunset, holding hands. Oh, my man, I love him so, he'll never know!! I am so, so grateful to God for giving a wonderful, loving soul mate and making all my dreams come true. Thank you, God!

Notice throughout this letter the author expresses how she feels. She describes in detail all aspects of her relationship including the home they share together and the time they spend including their sexual connection. When you read the letter, you can almost see it unfold like a movie.

Take the time to write your letter in vivid detail. Put it in an envelope and open it when you meet the person of your dreams. You will be amazed at how close your new love relationship will be to what you have written. This exercise is called Scripting and it is a very powerful tool to bring you the love of your life.

Now that you know what you want, it is time for you to start looking for the love of your life. You can find him/her anywhere. If you have done the work, you will be able to find them.

CHAPTER 16

Being a Great Talent Scout

There Must Be Fifty Ways to Meet Your Lover

This is the part you've been waiting for: Where do you meet eligible singles? Now that you know what you want in an ideal mate, we're going to share the answer to a common question: Where do you find him or her? When duck hunting, go where the ducks go. When you are looking for singles, go where the singles go.

One of the most common questions we get is "How did you meet each other?" The reality is we were both ready to meet each other. The "how" is just logistical. We both had done all the pre-work we are encouraging you to do. Unknowingly, we were preparing to be together as a couple. We had both become solid in who we were as individual people and were comfortable in our own skin. We knew what we wanted in our ideal mate. Both of us had our lists. Logistics wasn't really as important. But for those of you who just need to know:

Cupid reveals Jeannine and Keith's Love Story

Jeannine returned to college at age thirty-seven. It was her first day on campus as she began her long awaited journey to finish her college degree. She had a very successful career without a college degree but she had a never-ending desire to finish something that she had started at age eighteen. Life got in the way and she had never finished her bachelor's degree. On the first day of school, during her first coffee break, she saw an attractive man in the break room. He was dressed in a gray suit, white shirt and burgundy tie. Yes! She noticed him. That man was Keith!

As they reached for the coffee pot at the same time, there was a flirty interaction. They chatted, put cream and sugar in their coffee and sat down to relax. More flirting occurred. At that moment, they didn't realize that they had started the beginning of something wonderful.

Keith was teaching part-time at the college as an adjunct faculty professor. He was sitting in on a class to see if he might be interested in teaching it next semester. He had always taught at the college's main campus in San Francisco. Because his work load in his "real job" had increased he wanted to teach classes closer to home and this campus was considerably closer to his home.

Keith and Jeannine saw each other on campus several times more. One day, Keith was looking at the bulletin board in the break room and noticed a flier announcing a social gathering after class for both teachers and students. Jeannine was the person who had posted the flyer. Keith decided to attend. He thought it might be a good opportunity to talk Jeannine again. Jeannine and Keith believe that it was fate that they were the only two people to show up for this gathering. They spent hours talking. This meeting was the beginning of the wonderful friendship that forged Jeannine and Keith's amazing relationship. They were married three years later on Valentine's Day.

You will have your own story. There has never been a better time to be single. Things have really changed since the invention of the Internet. There are hundreds of thousands of available singles at your fingertips. But what is the best way to meet your future life partner? Internet dating is just one-way to meet singles but there are many other avenues for finding that love relationship.

When you are over thirty, you need to start looking for single people in different places than when you were in your twenties. Finding love in mid-life is different than finding love when we were younger. Remember, when you were young and everywhere you looked there were single people. You went to a party and there were single people in droves. Going to a bar, there were single people on every bar stool. During high school and college, almost everyone on campus was single. You didn't need to make much of an effort because available single people were all around you. As more and more of your friends got married, there were less single parties to go to on the weekends. The bar crowd started attracting the unattractive. On a day-to-day basis, you were no longer in school surrounded by like-minded singles. Did the well of singles dry up? Absolutely not!

For those of you who are complaining that there aren't enough single people to choose from, your focus is all wrong. First of all, there is a huge pool of single people in the United States. According the U.S. Census Bureau, in 2005, there were 89.8 million singles in the United States alone. This is 41% of the population over 18 years old. If you are a senior citizen, there is a huge population of senior singles. There is a whopping 14.9 million singles over 65 years old.

Let's think about this for a minute. If you line up 100 people, chances are, almost half of these people are going to be single. So there is a huge "well" of available singles. Keep this in mind because almost anywhere you go and whatever you are doing there is a strong possibility that you could meet "the one" if that's where your focus is.

After getting divorced, both of us simply went back to what we knew in our twenties, hanging out at our old stomping grounds. When we ventured out into the dating world, we gravitated to some of our old hang outs and discovered that not much had changed in the many years we had been out of the singles scene. Some of the same people we had done "shots" with when we were twenty-one were still sitting on the same bar stools. That should have been a really good clue that bars were not the place to meet our ideal mate. It took us a while to come to that conclusion.

So what are some better venues for finding your ideal mate? We are really going to stretch you out of your comfort zone. We want you to think about all the possibilities. Mr. or Ms. Right might knock on your door, but the probability is slim to none. If you really want to meet the right person, you are going to have to step it up a notch.

We are going to list some of our all-time favorite places to find quality singles. We want you to explore these venues with an open mind. If you say that you really want to be in a relationship with someone, you are going to have to muster up some courage and get out there.

We want you to think for a moment about every major accomplishment you have achieved in your lifetime. What did you have to do to get there? We are going to bet that you had to invest time, energy and money. In order for you to achieve your dream of finding your ideal mate, you are going to have to do the same thing.

What if you always do the least amount of work possible for something that you say is really important? The answer is, (drum roll please), you won't get the result you desire! If you aren't investing at least two hours per week into getting out and meeting singles, you are really not invested in the process. You need to go all out if you want the result of finding your ideal mate.

Most of the single people we meet are not willing to invest the time, effort, energy or money into meeting people that might be potential mates. If you are serious about finding "the one," then that is what you must do. We are not talking about becoming some crazed obsessed person who has only one thing on their mind. But we are saying that you have to do some hard work.

Take the time to determine some venues that might appeal to you.

Put aside your need for instant gratification. Don't expect to go to an event and BOOM, you meet the right person. It isn't going to work like that for the vast majority of you. You have to go out, learn more about yourself and your needs first. But if you don't go out, you don't stand a chance at meeting "the one." The remainder of this chapter should provide a wealth of ideas for you to explore on your soul mate quest but these are only suggestions. We are sure that you can easily add to these ideas.

Dating & Relationship Seminars

Since you are one of the singles who is working on self-improvement, you are probably interested in finding a mate who is also committed to working on him/herself. One of the best ways of meeting someone who is doing work on themselves is by going to dating and relationship seminars. We have had many people who have come to our seminars end up in a great relationship.

Singles Parties

One of the fastest growing means of meeting singles is single parties organized by professional party promoters. What is nice about these events is that it gathers like-minded singles under one roof. Everyone is looking for an opportunity to meet someone. The cost to attend the events is low and they usually have mingling games that make it easier for you to approach someone you are interested in. To find events in your area "Google" singles events and your city name.

Sometimes, a singles party might feel like a junior high school dance. You remember, don't you? The boys were on one side of the room and the girls were on the other. You hoped that some boy would walk over and ask you to dance. Even though a singles party might feel somewhat like that, investigate them. Check out multiple singles parties to find the right atmosphere for you. Remember that there are new faces at each event. One time you may go and feel that there was no one for you. Don't be discouraged. The next time, the right person could walk through the door.

Dating Services

Dating Services have been around for a long time. They can be a great way to meet singles. Some of the services do background checks weed out those with a criminal history. The pictures posted are usually taken by the dating service, so you know they are current.

The thing you should keep in mind about dating services is that often you are working with sales people who are on commission. It is their job to get you to buy the most expensive package. The packages they show usually aren't the only packages available, so ask about other options. They would rather sell you something than nothing at all.

Some dating services have only one package available. These services usually don't negotiate on price but you can always try. If you don't ask for a discount, you definitely won't get one.

The best time to visit a dating service offering multiple packages is towards the end of the month. The sales representatives are trying to meet their sales quotas and are much more motivated to make a deal. Try to purchase the cheapest package so you can try out the services. If you keep saying "no," they will keep pushing and present other options. Check the Better Business Bureau's information before going to dating services. You need to be a smart consumer.

Never give the dating service your Social Security number before making your purchase. If you read the small print under your signature of the form you fill out, you are giving them permission to do a credit check on you. What you don't know is that several of these dating services run your credit history before you meet with the sales representative to determine if you have credit available on your credit cards to buy their services. The sales representative knows how much you can afford before meeting with you. After you make a purchase, the dating service does need your Social Security number to do a complete background check and criminal investigation.

Professional Matchmakers

The field of professional matchmakers is growing by leaps and bounds. What is unique about matchmakers is that they work with you on your specific desires. They do a search to find a person who meets those needs. It is a very personal service that saves you from having to do all the work. For someone who is really busy, this service is truly a blessing. But keep in mind, you still must "be the one to find the one" even if someone else is doing the looking.

Say you want to work with someone who has been a matchmaker for many years. Ask them about how they work and their philosophy about dating success. You want to know what they are going to do for you other than just give you a list of people to contact. Many matchmakers offer dating coaching as part of their package as well as and discounts to some wonderful dating and relationship educational programs to help you increase your chances for success.

Some matchmakers actually will do an active search for your ideal mate. This means that they look outside of their paying clients for your matches. This very personalized approach can be costly, but very successful. For the busy professional, this is an ideal way of searching for a mate.

Some less expensive matchmaking services provide you with matches from within their paying client base. They will not actively look for men/women outside of their database but the cost is a fraction of what you would pay a traditional matchmaker.

We've listed a couple of matchmaking companies below with our understanding of the services they offer. Please contact them directly for exact information.

It's Just Lunch

You can purchase two different packages from *It's Just Lunch*. Your package will include a set number of introductions for a flat fee. The cost of lunch or drinks is not included in the membership.

Once you purchase a package, you will meet with an *It's Just Lunch* matchmaking expert to complete your profile. They will explore what you desire in a life partner. *It's Just Lunch* will then arrange dates with other men/women clientele who closely match your requirements.

Before accepting a date, make sure you reiterate your desires and make sure that the date meets your requirements. Again, you must be a good consumer.

Table for Six

This matchmaking company has a unique dating platform. They are a combination of a dating service and matchmaking organization all rolled up into one.

On the dating services end of the business, instead of matching you with one person, you go on a group date. You have dinner with five other people; two who are your same sex and three of the opposite sex. You get to meet three potential dates at the same time, but you are also competing with two other men/women for their attention. On the other hand, your same sex dining colleagues may turn out to be people who can introduce you to other potential dates or accompany you to other singles events.

Table for Six also has a more expensive program that caters to people wanting more individual attention. The highly desirable one-on-one matchmaking program is available to those who are willing to pay the additional fee.

Your membership includes a set number of dinners out. The cost of the dinner is not included. You pay for your own meal. Again, make sure that the men/women who will be attending the dinner, meet your requirements.

Another very desirable feature offered by *Table for Six* is their fun social events calendar. You can sign up for some very exciting activities and meet other members. If you meet someone at the event you find interesting or intriguing, *Table for Six* will set up a date.

The Right One

This matchmaking company has been around since the 1980s and is tried and true. It combines the personal touch of matchmaking with the high-tech computerized Internet dating.

The Right One considers itself to be one of the first matchmaking organizations in the United States. Unlike other dating services established before Internet dating websites became popular, this company has kept up with the current trends the industry.

Most of *The Right One's* matchmaking centers are owned and operated by *The Right One's* corporate offices with only a few franchises. *The Right One* has successfully been buying back franchises in an attempt to standardize and control the quality of service to their clientele.

The Right One has a variety of matchmaking packages available to singles. You might purchase half a dozen matches with this company and you can take years to use up all your dates. They want you to be happy, so there is no "expiration date" on your membership. If you are unhappy with the quality of a match, they will make it right.

Because they have offices nationwide, *The Right One* can draw from multiple offices to find you "the right one."

Speed Dating

This activity can be very fun. You have to go in with the right frame of mind. Speed dating events gives you the opportunity to meet many people in a short period of time. You are just checking for a level of chemistry and compatibility. If you don't find someone of interest the first time, you can go, try it again. Remember, you are just looking for one person! This type of event gives you a great opportunity to practice asking questions to find commonality. You select the people you might be interested in dating. If the same person selects you, the speed dating company will give you the information to get in touch with that person. You can select as many people as you desire. You might get several dates out of a speeding dating event.

Meetup.com

This is an amazing website. You can search for groups in your area that are involved in almost any activity. You can also search for singles groups that get together for activities and parties. But there is more! You can search for people who play golf, bowl, skiing or do any other type of activity. This website gives you the opportunity to do what you love and meet new people.

Internet Dating

Internet dating is wonderful because it offers you the opportunity to meet thousands of potential partners in the privacy of your own home. New people are joining Internet sites every day.

The challenge with Internet dating is that people can hide behind the veil of a computer screen to be whoever they want to be. There are many honest people on the Internet. They post a current picture, are truly single and are answering the questions openly and honestly. But for those who aren't honest, you need a screening process. The internet can also be a breeding ground for predators as well.

- Don't respond to someone who doesn't post a picture. Many people who are married, are looking for a quick hookup for a sexual affair and don't want their husband's or wife's friends to spot them online. Some people aren't happy with their appearance and won't post a picture. Some are professionals who don't want their clients to see them online. (Not too many fall into this category.) There are a few who don't know how to post a picture. But if their looks were a really big selling point, they would have someone help them. Our recommendation is: No picture, no response!

- Read the profile! Women are better about reading profiles than men. Men often look at the picture and then respond. Chemistry without compatibility is a recipe for disaster. Take the time to read the entire profile before you respond. Don't waste your time or their time. Yes, this is a numbers game but a calculated numbers game is more successful.

- If you have emailed back and forth three times without getting asked out, move on girls. Guys, if a girl won't go out with you after three or four good quality email exchanges, move on. Don't waste your time with people who are pumping up their egos through interacting with you. These people love soaking up the interest but they aren't willing to take action.

- Do not lie on your profile. You are going to get found out. Women lie about their weight most frequently, just like they do on their driver's license. Men tend to lie about height and career. Many people post a picture that is outdated or where they weighed less. Don't you want someone who will accept you for who you are? Then be honest! If you don't have a picture you like, invest in a professional photographer to take a good picture of you. Women really need to invest in a good picture because that is what men focus on. Put your best honest foot forward. Those professional glamour photos are pleasing to the eye but do you really look like that? You don't want to show up for a date and have him/her disappointed when they meet you. It is a waste of both of your time, (not to mention emotionally devastating.)

- When you write a profile, you want someone to get how you might fit into their life. Focus on activities that the opposite sex might be interested in doing with you. If you are a man who likes hunting, fishing and pistol shooting, think about how many women will like doing these activities exclusively. If you are a woman who likes needlepoint, decorating and crossword puzzles, how does a man fit into these interests? Instead, highlight activities such as boating, skiing, sailing, wine tasting and other less gender-specific interests.

- Don't answer any questions that make you feel uncomfortable on an Internet profile. Just because it is listed, doesn't mean you have to answer it.

- Never stay on a dating Internet site for more than a couple of months. Take your profile down and put it up on another site. Choose three sites you like and rotate through them at least every six months. Don't stay with one site more than two months. When your profile is considered NEW is when you will get the most activity. Get the most for your buck!! Rotate sites frequently. Contact the customer service number (usually found on your credit card statement) to cancel your subscription. Unless you do this, you may continue getting billed.

- Check out a number of dating Internet sites. There are thousands of dating sites available. Some are easier to navigate than others. A few of those sites are:

www.Perfectmatch.com

www.eHarmony.com

www.YahooPersonals.com

www.PlentyofDates.com

www.Matchmaker.com

All of these websites have value-added services and we have found them to be user-friendly and effective. You may find other websites that fit your needs better and we would love to get your feedback on them at cupidscoach@SMQmastery.com.

If you don't know whether you would enjoy Internet dating, you might check out Singlesnet.com or PlentyofFish.com or PlentyofDates. com because you don't have to pay any fees to be on these sites.

Single Activities and Clubs

One of the best ways to meet someone is by doing something you love. If you are a bowler, biker, hiker, golfer, rock climber, 4-wheeler, or ballroom dancer, look for single events focused around your interests and passions. Even if they are not specifically designated for singles, many singles will be attending just because they enjoy the activities.

Ski Clubs

There are many ski clubs for singles. They plan ski trips and usually have monthly mingling meetings even in the summer. So it isn't just about skiing, it is about socializing.

Cycling Clubs

There are also lots of cycling clubs around. Some are exclusively for singles. You want to make sure that the club you join has an opportunity for you to mingle. Make sure their plans include stops for lunch, coffee, or snacks on the outing. Otherwise, you won't have a chance to talk to anyone.

Golfing

Golf is a great way for to meet both women and men. If you don't golf, take some lessons. Get out on the driving range and keep your eyes open.

Book Clubs

You can start a book club and invite singles. You really get to know how someone thinks when you are discussing about what you both have read. Why not start a club that reads books about singles and have discussions about dating?

Singles Cooking Clubs

Someone told us that they started a singles cooking club. The club members got together every Sunday to prepare all their meals for the week together. They had single portioned meals to take home. We thought this was a great idea!

Bowling Club or Leagues

Call your local bowling alley and inquire into a singles league. Many bowling alleys have "singles" leagues or fun nights of "Disco Bowling."

Wine Tasting Clubs

If you like wine, a wine tasting club is a great place to meet other people of like interests. If there isn't one in your area, you can start one. Check with your local wine merchant. Many wine stores have wine tasting events on a regular basis.

Boating Clubs

If you like to motorboat or sail, check whether there is a singles boating club in your area. You don't need a boat. You can be one of the crew! Nearby marinas may have the information you need or check for groups on www.meetup.com by putting **boating** in the search subject line of the website!

Tennis Club

If you love tennis, then why not join a tennis club? They are usually inexpensive to join. Most tennis clubs have tournaments that last several day and these events include a lot of socializing. You can meet a lot of interesting people. At the very least, you'll meet a tennis partner.

Bring a Single Friend Party

This is one of our favorite ways for singles to meet new singles. Most of us have one or more single friend. You invite your single friends to the party and others do the same. The goal is to grow the group. Make everything simple and fun. You can meet at a park or rotate houses. Ask people bring appetizers, beer or wine. The hostess supplies the glasses and paper goods. You can just have it be a mixer or make each event fun by suggesting an activity like playing Pictionary, a wine tasting, karaoke or something else that is fun and interactive.

Church Singles Groups

Many churches have singles groups and events. These groups are not limited to just church members. They are usually open to the community. You are not guaranteed that a person you meet at one of these events will be from the same religious affiliation as the church. We recommend that you call and find out how many people usually attend these events and the age range of its participants. Go a few times and see if you connect with anyone. These are usually low cost or FREE events.

Church

In order to meet eligible singles through a church, you have to become more actively involved. Attending church activities such as festivals, bible studies, fundraisers, etc., will increase the possibility of meeting someone. Just attending services isn't going to open up many possibilities.

Volunteer

Get out there and do some volunteer work! If there is a cause you believe in, you will have that in common with the person you meet. You can become involved in a political campaign, an animal rights or rescue program. Whatever sparks your interest!

Self-Improvement Seminars

This is such a great place to meet lots of single females. Women are more likely than men to attend these types of seminars. The ratio of men to women gives men a wonderful opportunity to connect with a lot of women in a more intimate environment.

Financial Seminars

More men attend these types of seminars than women. Often there are opportunities to interact with others and have a chance to get to know someone on a different level. It never hurts to go to these seminars to take control of your investment or financial future. Many of these seminars are free or low cost.

Business/Industry Related Seminars

One area of commonality is work. You can meet someone who works in a similar field of work by attending industry-related seminars. Other business-related seminars, such as sales training, can be a way of meeting quality singles.

Chamber of Commerce/ Network Events

At a networking event, people are there to mingle and meet new people. It is expected. This makes it easy to introduce yourself to someone whom you find attractive. Bring lots of business cards!

Work

Some companies have a "no dating policy" for its employees, or seriously frown upon office romances. There is a reason for this. If a romance ends badly, it is difficult or impossible for both people to remain working together. *Before you have an office romance with a co-worker, examine whether your job is worth the risk. If you are dating a client, can you afford to lose their business if the relationship comes to a messy end? Some people do meet their husband or wife at work, but we would strongly encourage exploring other avenues.

*If you work for a big company and the person works in another department, it is much more acceptable to date in the workplace.

The Set-Up

Being introduced to someone by a mutual friend or someone else close to you (family, business associate) is a great way to meet someone. If you ask someone to set you up, give them your Top Ten relationship list. That will help them understand what you are looking for in a date. Always be kind to a person you are dating through an introduction. You don't want to ruin your relationship with someone close to you because you were a jerk.

Ballroom Dancing

Couples dancing is making a huge comeback! We think that every man should take ballroom dancing lessons. When you are good on the dance floor, women notice. Why do you think that women have loved movies like *Dirty Dancing, Saturday Night Fever* and shows like

Dancing with the Stars? Check around for weekly events for swing dancing, line dancing, tango or the salsa. It is okay to go alone and dance with people you meet there.

Sporting Events

Where can you meet thousands of people who are intent on having a darn good time? Any sporting event! It does not matter if it is baseball, basketball, football, soccer, hockey, beach volleyball or tennis. When people get together to support a professional or college sports team, the environment is emotionally charged with excitement. And here is the really good news; you already have something in common! You are fans and you are watching the game or the match.

Basketball and hockey game tickets can be pretty expensive. You can always purchase tickets in the cheap seats but buy your snacks near the more expensive seats. Make sure you dress to impress. Leave the baseball cap and sneakers at home. You can wear jeans but make sure you wear something that keeps you from blending into the crowd. Don't get decked out in fan attire from head-to-toe. It is not an attractive look.

The Gym

There are lots of singles who go to the gym. The best time to meet singles at the gym is in the morning before work or in the evening. Some people go to the gym at lunch, but they are usually in a rush to get through their workout in the limited time they have.

Cooking Classes

Men, this is another great venue for meeting women. And it sure doesn't hurt to know how to cook. Many high-end grocery stores offer cooking classes. Also, check with your community center because they often offer cooking classes, too. Choose a fun class such as how to make pizza or dim sum.

Senior Centers

If you are in your senior years, you can meet some great people through senior centers. They have lots of activities that encourage interaction. You can't really lose! You can have fun and meet interesting people with whom you can socialize. Don't think for a minute that you will find a group of elderly people sitting around in their wheelchairs playing bingo. Senior centers encourage seniors to live an active life!

College Classes or Adult Education

We are partial to this way of meeting. After all, this is how we met. Even if you don't find the love of your life, it is never too late to get more education. You can take classes in a subject that interest you at your local community college. Just for fun, pick up a current college course catalog and scan through your options. You never know who you will meet when you go back to school.

Personal Ads

Many people still use personal ads to meet that special someone. Some post their personal ads in newspapers and others will post them on internet sites like Craig's List. Either way, there is very little information available in a personal ad. Make sure that you are careful when meeting someone you have connected with via these dating venues. Because there is so much anonymity, you should take safety precautions. Again, be aware of predators.

- **Make sure you meet in a public place.**

- **Don't invite them to your home. This includes picking you up for a date. Wait until you have met three or four times and feel like you know them better.**

- **A secondary precaution is to always let someone know where you are going, when you expect to return and any information you** know about the person you are intending to meet, including their phone number and email address. We call this a "Safety Net."

You must call your "Safety Net" when you return from your date or if you are running later than expected. Be consistent about doing this. If you ever fail to call, your "Safety Net" will know that there is a problem and can take immediate action.

Book Stores

Many bookstores now have places to sit and look at books or magazines while making your selection. Our favorite places to hang out are the periodical and self-improvement sections. We love people who are interested in self-development. What are your interests? Go hang out in that section of the book store and author reading events. Most bookstores have book clubs. These offers great ways another way to meet people who share your interest in reading.

Grocery Stores

Many singles like to shop later in the evenings to avoid the crowds, moms with toddlers, full grocery carts and coupon-clipping retirees. Try going to the store at different times and observing the people shopping. You might just be reaching for the milk at the same time as the love of your life. Many singles go to the prepared food section or deli section of the grocery store. They are looking quick meals in single portions. Keep your eyes open.

Weddings

People are in the mood for love at weddings. Many people have told us that they met their mates at a wedding. However, we want to make it clear that we do not encourage wedding crashing. Make sure you are dressed to impress. You want to stand out in the crowd.

Class Reunions

Many people rekindle an old love at a reunion. There is so much commonality with people who have gone to school together. What is your old crush up to? You never know!

Charity Events

What a great way to meet a giving, caring person. If you go to support an event or cause that you believe in, you might just find the right person. Wouldn't it be wonderful if you shared the same passion?

New Year Eve Parties

A lot of people make it their New Year's goal to meet the right person. But the night itself can offer the chance to make that goal come true. New Year's Eve abounds with festive gatherings. You don't have to go them alone. Get a group of friends to welcome in the New Year with you. Some of these events can be pricey, but what the heck. Even if you don't meet the love of your life, you've gotten the New Year off to a fun start!

Halloween Parties

When people are dressed up in costume, they are much more fun. This is an opportunity to don a disguise and step into a different character for a single night. You can be a bit wacky and it is perfectly acceptable. If you are a bit shy, a Halloween party might just be the venue to let your inner child come out and play.

Car / Motorcycle Races

You will meet a lot of men and women at the racetrack. They are usually in a good mood and open to adventure. This is a haven for single women seeking adventurous single men. Dress up girls! You are going to have to do a little work to get a man's attention away from the fast moving vehicles.

Car Shows

We've observed that at car shows, it seems to be raining men! This is a paradise for women seeking single men. Often in autumn or late summer, major cities will have a car show sponsored by car manufacturers so they can display their new models to the public. Other car shows might feature antique or classic cars for you to check out along with their owners.

Boat Shows

There were many men at the recent boat show we attended but there were a lot of women, too. It seems that boats and beautiful people go hand in hand. The boats are good conversation starters. You can view sailboats, racing boats and yachts. Who knows! Soon you might be sailing with a new love interest.

Horse Races

Again, you will meet a lot of men at the horse races and many of them will be willing to help a novice place her first bet. Just be careful not to fall for a fellow with a gambling addiction.

The best time to go to the track is when it holds a party to celebrate a race like the Kentucky Derby. You will not be able to see the actual race live but your can enjoy the festivities while you watch the race on the big-screen television. Women, if you are attending a Kentucky Derby party, you must wear a hat. It is a long-standing tradition.

Single Cruises

Many cruise lines have single cruises. Check with a cruise line to find out the age group of their single cruises. It would be disappointing to be mismatched with the other passengers. What if you found yourself on the geriatric love boat when you want to be on the booze cruise? Or worse, what if you were surrounded by youngsters partying like Spring Break when you want to play bridge and shuffle board? Something else to consider is departing from a "port of call" that is close to your home. If you travel across the country to catch your cruise ship, chances are you will be dealing with a long distance relationship if you meet the love of your life on the ship. Don't be cheap about choosing a cruise. The more upscale the cruise line, the more upscale the clientele.

Hardware Stores

Yes, you can meet men at the hardware store. But most of the men we have seen there seem to be very focused on their purchase and not the single women in the store. You would do better to enroll in a "Do It Yourself" class at the store where you are more likely to catch their attention.

Dog Parks

A friend of ours likes to go to the dog park with her Golden Retriever. When she sees a good looking man with a dog, she will strike up a conversation about his dog by saying something like, "You have a German Shepard. Are those good family dogs?" She quickly finds out if they are married or have children. We think it is brilliant. If you can win over a person's dog, you have a chance at winning their heart.

Bars

Many people think that bars are a great way to meet singles. We are going to put this method of meeting quality singles at the bottom of the list. The reason is that many people in bars are newly out of relationships and not really ready for a new relationship, or they have never left the bar scene. Either way, the probability of meeting the right person is slim. But we can't rule it out. We've heard of people meeting the love of their life in a bar.

Night Clubs

The club scene is simply another way of saying a bar. They are a great place to practice flirting, but you probably won't meet the right person there. However, some clubs specialize in certain types of live music like jazz or Indie rock. Sharing on interest in music is a good conversational starting point.

It doesn't matter how many venues we throw at you. If you don't get out and mingle, you won't be successful. Is there the possibility that Mr. or Ms. Right will knock on your door? Yes! What are the probabilities? Slim!!! So, you need to get off your fanny and start mingling to find the right person.

The love of your life can come into your experience in a number of ways. They might be the person you meet in the checkout line at the local grocery store. They might be the person who comes to repair your refrigerator or deliver a package to your work or home. But, if you get out and mingle with singles, you will have a much better chance of meeting that special person.

CHAPTER 17

Getting Your Flirt On

When we say that you need to learn to flirt, we get a lot of resistance from singles. You would think we asked them to do a strip tease in the middle of Central Park! Most people think of flirting as something sexual and alluring. Nothing can be further from the truth.

We are both big flirts, but not the kind of flirting that you might consider sexual. The flirting we are referring to is really quite simple. We really care about people and we like to engage in conversation to learn about them. We ask people about their lives and listen intently to what they say. We also are able to engage in insignificant, small talk chats with most people, too.

Flirting is simply connecting with someone. It doesn't even matter what you are connecting about. You can connect with someone in the supermarket while standing in the checkout line by asking them if they like a certain type of cleaning product or salad dressing or sauce they are buying. Most people are very helpful and generous if given the opportunity. Because flirting isn't sexual in any way, it isn't threatening to most people. Now, if you ask someone in the grocery line how they like the Trojan condoms they are buying, well, that might be considered sexual and weird. But, let's get real here. There aren't too many items in the grocery store that would be considered sexual. So flirt away!

Two of the best books on flirting are written by Susan Rabin and Barbara Lagowski. *How to Attract Anyone, Anytime, Anyplace: The Smart Guide to Flirting* and is a best seller. We also recommend their book *101 Ways to Flirt: How to Get More Dates and Meet Your Mate*. Susan Rabin is internationally recognized as a leading expert on Flirting. Visit her website **www.SchoolofFlirting.com** for more information on her insightful flirting seminars.

If you are not a natural flirt, you need to practice flirting before you step out and try to make a love connection at a singles event. The more comfortable you are with making a connection with someone in the outside world, the better you will be in a room of singles. The world is your classroom. Learn what works for you. Have some fun flirting. It is just clean fun.

Another way of flirting is giving someone a sincere compliment. We have made people's day just by noticing something about them and giving them a sincere compliment. Everyone likes getting a compliment.

Next, we would like to distinguish between flirting and what we call "hunting." Hunting is sexual in nature. Hunting consists of those alluring gestures that let someone know that you are really interested in them on a sexual level. Hunters do things like bat their eyes, touch someone's arm or leg, lean in and whisper something in someone's ear, send over a drink hoping to get someone's attention.

If you want someone to be attracted to you for reasons other than sex, don't lead with sexual innuendo using provocative behaviors or words to snag a date. People who attempt to attract the opposite sex through sexually allure are "on the hunt," not flirting. Like a predator hunting prey, people who hunt are more interested in the conquest. Hunting is about meeting a single person's needs, not both.

There are natural flirts and flirting comes as easily to them as brushing their teeth. These people learned at a young age that connecting with people felt good. A young child might smile at people in church or waved to strangers on the street and beam when they returned the attention. If you didn't get your flirting practice as a kid, you need to kick it up as an adult if you want to be successful in dating. You have to practice.

EXERCISE: Turning on Your Inner Flirt

Here is a great practice exercise for flirting. Before you leave the house in the morning, take three pennies and put them in your left pocket of your pants or jacket. The goal is to flirt with three people during the day. Every time you flirt with someone, you get to move a penny into your right pocket. You can't end the day until all three pennies are in your right pocket. You can flirt with a person of any sex or age. It doesn't matter. By doing this exercise, you will be much more comfortable flirting with available singles where ever you might meet them.

Young children are so fun to interact with. They love getting a compliment. But then they play this cute coy game of hiding behind their parent and peeking out to see if you are still noticing them. Another way great way to flirt is give couples a compliment on how well-behaved their children are in a restaurant. People notice children who are misbehaving but not many notice children who are well-mannered. You can make the parents' and children's day with your compliment.

The more you flirt in the real world, the better you will be in a singles environment. Remember, the world is your classroom and laboratory. The more you flirt, the better you become at the process.

Make a commitment to yourself to practice flirting for a month. At the end of that month, you will be an expert flirter. You will be ready to go to any singles event and connect with someone.

How to Mingle At A Singles Event

Earlier in the book we reminisced about junior high school dances where the girls sat on one side of the room and the boys on the other. Either you sat patiently and waited for someone to ask you to dance or tried to muster up enough courage to ask someone to join you on the dance floor. Going to a singles event can feel the same way.

A singles event can be very stressful, or it can be extremely fun. Our goal is to help you take the edge off of mingling at singles events. We are going to walk you through the entire process, step by step.

The more you get out there and practice, the better you will become at mingling. If you aren't willing to take some risks, you just might be setting yourself up to spend the remainder of your life alone.

If you make just a few small changes in your flirting and mingling, you can change your results. If a ship sailing from New York to England changes its course by just one degree, it will end up in a different country. What can you do to change your course by one degree so you can end up in a different place in your love life?

We really want you to go into this process with an open mind and the belief that you have a much higher probability of finding the right person if you are willing to take a leap of faith. Great love is found by taking a risk and having faith that you will have a favorable outcome.

Going to singles events is something we do weekly. We have to keep our pulse on what is going on in the singles' world in order for us to be effective dating coaches. What we observe attending these events really makes our toes curl.

Often, we see people sitting against the wall completely out of sight of other singles in the room. They couldn't make it harder for someone to approach them if they tried. Others sit at tables with their arms crossed and sourpuss looks on their faces. This makes them even more unapproachable.

One of our clients, Sylvia, is very successful at engaging men when she goes to singles events. She comes to the event with a smile on her face and a spring in her step. We see her stand close to the dance floor and enjoying the music by swaying her body to the rhythm of the music. In no time, she is on the dance floor. Her dance card is always full. Sylvia considers each event to be a success because she had a good time.

Your attitude paves the road for you to enjoy and feel successfully at singles events. We will share some of our secrets that will jumpstart you into the process and if applied will increase your chances of success.

Get Ready for The Event

You always want to look your best when you go to a singles event. When you look great, you feel great! Take the time to pick out an outfit that is flattering. You might even want to go out and purchase some dating clothes. We recommend that women wear tomato red or something in the coral color family. Men are attracted to these colors. The worst dating colors for women are aqua and pink. Women find these colors attractive but men don't. Men should wear blue. The richer the blue color, the better. Women are attracted to blues. This will help you stand out in a crowd and get noticed.

Take the time to make sure you hair looks good. If you need a haircut get one before you go. Make sure your shoes are polished and your nails are well-manicured. These are little things but they can ruin whole look and make you appear unkempt.

Women should get a business card printed with their first name, email address and phone number. If someone asks you for your phone number, you will be able to give them your "calling card." You can make these cards on your computer. If you don't know how to do this, then go to www.VistaPrint.com. Vista Print will print your calling cards for FREE! Check it out.

Use only your first name on the card. You should not give out personal information until you know someone better.

Some people like to put their picture on the card so the person receiving the card remembers them.

We recommend setting up an email account just for dating. Make sure that your email address doesn't reveal personal information about you like your city or last name.

Some people set up a separate voicemail box with a phone number just for dating. You need to check your voicemail everyday if you've given someone your phone number. Search the Internet to find the best service for you or get a free voicemail box at Simple Voice Box: 877-482-5838 or at **www.OneBox.com.**

Mingle or Remain Single

You can go to a singles event by yourself or go with a friend. Men are more likely to go to a singles event solo than a woman. Just because you do not have anyone to go with to the event should not keep you from going.

When you get to the event, find yourself a seat somewhere in the middle of the room and with a view of the door, if possible. This gives you a great opportunity to see who is coming in the room. However, you will be spending very little time in your chair. Moving around the room is what gives you the greatest opportunity to meet the people in the room. And that's why you're there!

Go get yourself a drink. The drink table or bar is a great place to start the mingling process. Having a drink in your hands also prevents you from crossing your arms. Body language experts stress that crossing your arms indicates that you do not want to be approached. You appear uncomfortable, bored and guarded. Watch your body language.

Get to know the bartender. Being on a first name basis with the bartender is always good for getting drinks quickly and you can appear to be in the know by using an opening line to meet someone like: "Barry the bartender makes a wonderful cosmopolitan. Have you tried one?" Also, tipping the bartender generously the first time you order a drink will greatly increase your opportunity to get the bartender's attention later in the evening when there is a larger crowd attempting to get drinks.

Level One: Risk-Free Opening Lines

Having a few good opening lines will keep you relaxed when attending a singles event or party. You don't need a whole slew of them. Look over our ideas and choose a few opening lines that feel comfortable for you. Some of these lines are risk-free. Some of the lines are funny and others are ballsy. Use the lines that best suit you.

"Excuse me. I hope you don't mind me coming up to you out of the blue. I don't know anyone at this party. My name is..."

"How did you learn about this Singles Event?"

"How do you know the host or hostess?"

"How is life treating you?"

"Doesn't (use the hostess/host name) look great tonight?"

"This music reminds me of my childhood [high school days/college days]. How about you?"

"So what was YOUR day like today?"

"I just can't believe how beautiful/dark/noisy/crowded it is here! Can you?"

"Isn't this [type of food you are eating or have tried] delicious?"

"I just love this place. Have you been here before?"

Notice that each one of these lines requires a response. They are simple and non-threatening.

Level Two: The Playful Line

If you are more experienced at mingling or have an outgoing gregarious personality, you might want to step it up a bit and try some of these playful lines. Don't eliminate a line because it doesn't work the first time. Try it a few times.

"Am I interrupting something confidential?"

"Excuse me, but what is that wonderful-looking thing you're eating/ drinking?"

"Hello! I'm practicing my mingling tonight. How am I doing?"

Level Three: The Daring Line

These are a lot more daring but oh so much more fun. It isn't what you say, but how you say it. You might want to practice these in front of a mirror before using them in public. Check out your facial expression and say these lines with confidence so you may carry them off.

"Okay guys, what's the password over here?"

"I've been told that I should come and talk to you. I can't tell you who sent me; I'm sworn to secrecy."

"Excuse me, but my friend bet me I couldn't walk up to you and immediately start talking... no, don't look at her!... please just smile -- that's good -- and talk to me so she/he has to buy the drinks tonight."

How to Join a Group

When you are at a singles event and want to join in a conversation of a group, follow some simple guidelines to be more successful in the process.

Larger Group (4 or More)

Watch for the body language of a group. When people are standing closer together, it shows they have some level of familiarity. These groups are harder to break into and blend in. Look for more loosely formed groups.

Don't introduce yourself and shake hands with a large group. You will disrupt the flow of the group. The goal is to blend into the group.

Listen to the conversation and wait for an opportunity to make a comment. You need to open your mouth and speak at some point.

Don't mingle with a buddy. It is harder for two people to blend into a group than one. Split up and meet people in the room. Then you can both introduce each other to the people you have met in the room.

Women have a harder time separating from their buddies than men. They hang out together, go to the ladies room together and go to the bar in unison. Can you imagine a man saying to his friend, "Do you need to go to the bathroom?" And the other guy says, "No, but I'll go with you anyway." Women, you need to separate from your "security blanket" friend and mingle!

Smaller Group (2-3 People)

When entering a smaller group of two or three, look for the same in body language cues we described for larger groups. If the people in the group are standing close together, they probably know each other pretty well. In a smaller group, it is appropriate to shake hands and make your introduction but it is not necessary.

Talking With an Individual

If you are a novice at mingling, you might want to look for someone who is standing alone and introduce yourself. However, it is harder to leave the conversation with an individual versus a group. But you will need to move on unless the person you are talking with really rocks your world.

Biggest Mistakes People Make at Singles Events

At most social events, alcohol is served. One big mistake people make is drinking too much. Limit your alcohol intake. Have one or two drinks and then switch to soda, juice or water. Drinking might loosen you up, but too much drinking can make you reckless and just annoying. No one likes talking to a drunk.

Your goal is to meet as many people as possible with the goal of trying to make a love connection. Staying with a group for too long interferes with this goal. To leave a group, you simply need to excuse yourself and go find other people to chat with. Here are some of the best ways to exit a conversation or group:

Excuse me. I have to get another drink.

Excuse me. I'm going to check out the food table. I'm starved.

Excuse me. I need to make a phone call

Excuse me. I need to find my friend.

Excuse me. I need to powder my nose.

Excuse me. I'm going to step outside for some fresh air.

Don't hang out at the food table or bar too long. This is a great place to start the mingling process but if people continue to hang out there, it will get really crowded. It is also really hard to talk with food in your mouth. Move on and move around the room.

Don't hang out with a friend the whole night. It makes you less approachable. This is one of the biggest complaints we get from men. Women hang out in cliques making it hard for a man to approach someone in the group. You are hurting your chances of meeting someone when you do this.

Don't plant yourself in one place all night. Move around the room. If you want to dance, stay near the dance floor and appear interested in the music. Try not to look like a deer in the headlights. If you look uncomfortable, you are not approachable. Keep a smile on your face and a spring in your step. People who appear to be having a good time are like magnets to other people.

Resist going to a singles event with a friend who always has to be in the spotlight. No matter what you do, you are going to be second fiddle. Try to go to the event with someone who is willing to step aside and disappear when you make a connection with someone. It is best that you discuss this ahead of time and have a code phrase that you both can use to give the other a signal. Some ideas are:

Did you get a hold of the babysitter to check in?

Did they find your sunglasses? You might want to check again!

It looks like a good time to get a drink. There aren't too many

>   *people in the drink line.*

If you flub up by saying something embarrassing or inappropriate have a line ready for that situation. Learn to laugh at yourself and make light of mistakes. Our favorite lines are:

Can we rewind that?

Did I say that out loud?

Let's run that scene over again.

Excuse me. My alter ego just took over my body for minute.

Avoid talking about politics, religion, sex or your ex. There are plenty of things to talk about without opening those cans of worms.

Some Other Good Ideas

Practice mingling. The more you mingle, the better you will get. If you are shy, use a wingman. That is where a more outgoing friend who will approach someone you are interested in, start a conversation and then introduce you. The wingman then exits to use the restroom and leaves you two to talk.

Practice your opening lines in front of a mirror so you see your facial expression. A great deal of what we convey is through body language. Body language can signal fun and playfulness.

Practice flirting outside of a singles event so you get good at it. Flirting is simply making small talk with someone you don't know. You can do it anywhere and with anyone. It isn't sexual or alluring. It is simply making a friendly connection with someone.

The more you get out and practice mingling, the better you will get at it. You will get more comfortable the more often and frequently you attend singles events. If finding a life partner is one of your highest goals in life, you have to put in the time to make it happen. If you are putting in an hour a week finding your ideal mate and that is one of your highest priorities, there is something wrong. The time you spend needs to be proportionate to your level of desire to obtain your goal.

CHAPTER 18

Getting In the Game by Creating Great Dates

Now that we have defined your ideal mate and identified places and resources to find single people, it is time to move into the dating process.

Let's define a date. A date is a targeted opportunity to get to know someone. You are trying to determine if this person has the potential to be a life partner. Most people don't maximize the information gathering purpose of the date. They have superficial conversations that don't get them any closer to finding out if a person is a potential match. This can waste precious time! You can be three months or more into the dating process with someone before you find out if that person is a great match for you, or you can find it out on the first few dates. The reality is that the answers are going to be the same whether you ask the questions on the first few dates, or six months later. So the question to you is: Do you want to know the answer sooner or later?

First dates can be a little stressful and awkward. You are entering the mind, heart and world of another person without a map. If initiating a conversation is difficult for you, you might want to put together a list of potential conversations starters and memorize them. On a first date, keep the conversation light. Subjects like religion, politics, sex and marriage are not good first date subjects. Start discussing these subject matters around the third date.

You can cut down on the awkwardness of a first date by doing some preparation. Think of subjects that would be mutually interesting to both you and your date. Some of our favorite conversation starters are:

Where did you grow up?

Do you have any brothers and sisters?

Did you go to college?

What do you like to do for fun?

Do you like to travel?

Where is your favorite place to go?

These light subjects will give you a lot of good information about your date and will get the conversation rolling. Add them to your list and have a variety of conversations starters that will keep the conversation moving. Remember, this is not an interview, it is a date!

So once you are past the conversations starters, where do you go? We have a great list of questions for you. These will make the process so much easier. Here is our suggestion:

EXERCISE: Conversation Starters

Make an index card with some of your favorite questions and keep them in your purse, wallet or on your cell phone. If you get stuck on a date and are looking for something to ask, you will have the questions at your fingertips. Go to the bathroom, look at your list and then return to your date with some fresh ideas.

You might not be comfortable asking all of the questions on our list. That is okay. Pick the ones that feel right to you. Some people are more comfortable asking bolder questions. Others are more conservative and don't want to step on anyone's toes. Both are fine. However, the person who is bold will get a lot more information much more quickly.

Up Your Game By Asking Bolder Questions!

The more you step it up, the more successful you will be in the dating world. You are looking for compatibility. The more you learn about your date, the better equipped you will be to decide if you want to continue dating, or end it and say "next!" Don't waste your time with someone who isn't a good match for you. Some people will just date someone because they would rather be with anyone, than be alone. That really isn't fair to you and it certainly isn't fair to your date. Dating to find your ideal mate does not consist of filling up your time on pointless dates. You can, and should, spend your time more wisely.

Now, some people who may make the decision to discontinue dating someone because they leaped to an inaccurate conclusion about something their date said. If you aren't sure about something your date says, ask a follow up question.

Have you ever concluded after a first date that the person wasn't right for you? A friend of ours once did not want to go on a second date with a man based on their first date. We had to push her to give him a second chance. He worked in a blue-collar industry, a refinery, and she was determined to date someone who had a professional job, or a white-collar worker. She had dated several men who worked in blue-collar jobs and she felt that she did not have much in common with them. She wanted someone who worked in the corporate world like herself.

On her second date with this man, our friend learned that he was in fact a white-collar worker in a blue-collar world. He was in upper management at the refinery. She almost missed out on someone who was a great match because she misunderstood what he did for a living and didn't ask a clarifying question to learn more.

Here is another near miss with the same dating relationship. Our friend was on a date with her new love interest and he mentioned that he was going to a big, family, Fourth of July party. She responded by saying that she didn't go to many family events. Her new boyfriend mistakenly concluded that meant she didn't like going to family events. His ex-wife had refused to go to family functions, so this man now knew that he really wanted someone who would like going to family events. He almost dumped our friend. Because he really liked her, he took the time to ask her more questions about why she didn't go to family functions. Imagine his surprise when he learned that our friend is an orphan. Her only living relative is one brother so family events are few and far between. She actually hoped to find someone who would invite her to his family's functions.

When our friend and her love interest finally talked about their near misses, they had a good laugh. They both had really initially misunderstood each other. Without further communication it could have been a disaster!

Don't draw hasty conclusions! If you find yourself creating a story about what you think someone has said, ask a question and clarify. You might just miss out on the best thing that has ever happened to you if you don't.

We are going to share some of our top dating questions with you. Remember, these questions are geared toward finding your ideal mate. You might not like some of them but try them on for size and see what happens. You never know. A question that seems strange to you might become your very favorite question. Be prepared to answer these questions yourself. We call this, "The Boomerang Effect." Your date more often than not will ask, "How about you?"

The Serious Questions:

- *What are you most proud of in your life?* This tells you a lot about someone. Are they happy with their accomplishments? Was it hard for them to come up with one? Was it because there were too many or too few?

- *Where do you see yourself in five years time?* Is this a goal-oriented person? Do they think at all about their future? You might hear what you want to hear--that they would like to be married.

- *What three words would your best friend use to describe you?* This is a good question because it makes your date look at themselves through someone else's eyes.

- *If you had only six months to live, what would you do?* This is a great question for uncovering what someone values in life.

- *Who are you closest to in your family and why?* You can gain some insight into their family relationships with this one tiny little question.

- *If you could choose any career for yourself, what would you choose?* You can learn a lot about someone's desires and passions by asking this question. Why they didn't end up in their chosen career might be really insightful, too.

- *What is something that makes you unique or special?* Now we are getting down to some meat! Do they have healthy self-esteem? Are they arrogant?

- *If you could pass on one piece of wisdom to the world, what would it be?* You can really get into someone's head with this question!!!

- *If you could have one "do-over" in life, what would it be?* We learn the most from our mistakes. You can almost bet that they have learned something from this life mistake.

Commonality & Compatibility Questions

- *Are you an outdoor or an indoor person and what do you enjoy about that?* This is a great question to uncover commonality. If you are an indoor person and they like the great outdoors, you are going to have some problems spending time together.

- *Where in the world would you most like to be this weekend and why?* Do you both like going to the same kind of places? You could uncover a great place to go for a weekend retreat if you develop a relationship.

- *What is your favorite morning beverage?* This is kind of like finding out if they wear boxers, briefs or bikini underwear. More a fun question than a crucial one.

- *How would you describe a perfect Sunday morning?* Does the person hop out of bed to make it to church? Or is he or she a slow riser who reads the newspaper until noon? Do they like going out for Sunday brunch? Do they go for a run in the morning? What are their Sunday morning rituals? This question offers you great insight into their life.

- *If you could live anywhere in the world where would it be?* This is a great opportunity to see if they have thought about living somewhere else in the world and why. They might reveal that they once lived in another place and would love to move back there. Who knows?

- *What makes you laugh?* What in life do they think is funny or cute enough to make them laugh?

- *What makes you cry?* What evokes the emotion of crying? Is it a movie, the loss of something or someone? What makes them tick?

- *What is your favorite type of music and/or favorite band?* Of course this important. You don't want to fight over the radio station on a road trip.

- *Do you have any pets?* You might find out they are allergic to cats and you would never part with your cat, Fluffy.

- *Are you a morning person or a night person?* If your body clocks are complete opposites, when will you have quality time together?

- *Which TV program would you never miss?* You know who will be controlling the remote at that time.

- *Who is your favorite athlete?* It is interesting to find out who someone admires and why. Does he or she follow sports or would you have to dragging them kicking and screaming to see your favorite team play?

- *What is your favorite sporting activity?* Is there an activity you can do together? Do they golf, boat, or ski? Would you be interested in watching them participate in their sport?

Lighthearted Questions

- *Who was your hero as a child?* This is just a fun question and a trip down memory lane. It can trigger some great conversations about your childhoods.

- *What did you want to be when you grew up?* This gives you have a lot more to talk about. You can ask about how they got into their profession or what changed their mind about their childhood career fantasy.

- *If you could be successful at any job in the world, what would you do?* This question will reveal their hidden passion about career. You might even learn that they are working in the perfect job.

- *What is your favorite season and why?* It is just fun to get into their likes and dislikes. We personally like summer because we love being outdoors. If they like summer, why?

- *If you could have lunch with any person, living or dead, who would it be and why?* Uncovering who they admire or whom they would want to ask some powerful revealing questions can give you some good insight to their character.

- *If you could time-travel to the past to correct any mistakes you feel you've made, would you?* What do they consider a mistake? This unveils their thoughts about what experiences in life have made them the person they are today. There is a lot to this question.

- *If you won the lottery, how would you spend your millions?* It is fun to fantasize. You can get some great information on their dreams and how they handle money. You might also learn whether they are philanthropic and what causes they feel are important enough to support with donations.

- *If money was no object, what frivolous thing would you buy?* How fun is this question? What is that one thing that has eluded them?

- *What was the first music recording you ever bought?* Another trip down memory lane that can reveal commonality about music likes and dislikes.

- *What luxury item would you take on a desert island?* It is fun to find out what luxury items they value and their thought process. (If she says a hair dryer for a desert island, you might want to check out her overall intelligence.)

- *If you have friends coming for supper what would you cook?* This reveals a lot about how they like to entertain and if they even can cook. If you love to entertain, this is a great question to ask. Maybe you don't cook. If they don't cook either, you just might starve.

- *What is one food you would never eat?* Let's hope it isn't Chinese food if that is your favorite.

- *If you could be someone else for a day, who would you be?* This is such a fun question because the possibilities are endless! You can uncover their fantasies. You might learn what they would do if they had another person's talent or personal power for a single day.

- *What did you do today that made you feel good?* This gives you insight into the things that make them happy.

- *What three things would you like me to know about you before the date is over?* This will give you great information right up front and some deep topics to talk about. You can ask additional probing questions to learn more about these three things.

- *Do you believe in love at first sight?* You are checking out their overall mind set. Are they a romantic or are they a logical person?

- *What is your most treasured possession?* Are they sentimental? This offers great insight into what they value in life.

- *What is your favorite month of the year?* All kinds of facts can emerge from asking. You might find out their favorite holiday or you may discover what month their birthday falls.

- *What is your favorite book/movie?* This is a great question to help find commonality. You might even find out that they don't enjoy reading or watching movies.

- *What is the last book you read?* Does this person read on a regular basis or has this person not picked up a book since high school or college? If you love to read, belong to a book club or pride yourself on being well-read, this is worth checking out.

- *Who was your first crush?* This always fun and light. It could have been an actor or someone in their kindergarten class. Who knows? But typically you get to hear a cute story.

- *What is the most romantic thing you have ever done?* Buckle up! You never know what they are going to say. If you are looking for a true romantic and the most romantic thing they have ever done was buy a red rose, forget it!

- *What is the best date you have ever been on?* You might want to line up something similar in the future if you really want to turn her/him on.

- *What is the wackiest thing you have ever done?* How adventurous is this person? Is that important to you?

- *What was your favorite movie of all time?* This has got to be a good one. Chick flick, action adventure, science fiction, horror or kiddy film? Let's hope for everyone's sake it isn't a porn movie.

Beyond the First Date Questions

- *When was your last relationship and how long did it last?* You need to ask this question. Is the person a serial dater, commitment phobic or do they trade in their boyfriend/girlfriend for a new model often. You might even find out that they are still in a relationship and shopping around for their next conquest.

- *What are you looking for in a relationship?* If you aren't looking for the same thing, it is time to say "next."

- *What do you value most about being in a relationship?* This will give you some insight into the type of relationship that works for him/her.

- *Do you want to or have you ever been married?* This can reveal some major baggage or to find out if they even want to be married. If someone doesn't believe in marriage or marriage isn't something they are working towards, you need to know it. Don't waste time trying to convince someone that you are a good enough catch to change their ideas about marriage.

- *Do you want/do you have any children?* If you don't want children and they have children, you can't separate the package deal. If you want children and they don't, move on.

- *Why are you not in a relationship now?* You never know what you are going to get. A man we met when we were at a bar with a client who told us he was separated from his wife. As we talked more, he revealed that he was still living with his wife for the sake of the children. This guy was still married, not separated, but shopping around for a fling! He had no intention of leaving his wife. Some women might get sucked into this line of bull, but we saw it for what it was. He was just a cheater. That is good information to know because you don't want to date someone who is not available. You also don't want to date someone who doesn't have enough guts to break off a relationship with another person before shopping for someone new. This is cheating and who wants to be with a cheater?

The most important thing to remember when you are dating is to have fun! Keep the first couple of dates short. You don't want to get caught on a four or five hour date with someone who bores you. The two primary things you are looking for on the first couple of dates are chemistry and compatibility. So have fun asking questions. If you don't have a love connection, you will learn it early in the process and you can move on.

You have to be in an environment that allows you to ask these questions. It doesn't have to be the classic dinner and movie date. In fact, going to the movies leaves you very little opportunity to get to know each other. You might learn what kind of movies they like, but you are not going to "chat it up" during the movie unless you want someone in the theatre to throw their popcorn at you.

A date can be as simple as having a cup of coffee or a glass of wine together. Of course, it can also be more adventurous and fun. But we always recommend keeping it simple and staying close to home if at all possible for the first date. Plan to keep the date short. If the date is a bust you can end the date. If you are having a fabulous time, you might want to stay a bit longer.

CHAPTER 19

Avoiding First Date Fumbles

In speaking with singles, it seems that many think dating is a lot of "work." They complain about how much work it is to: find a date, look your best, make a good first impression, get to know people, play the dating game. Talk about sucking the fun right out of the dating process. We are here to put the fun back into the dating game. Are you willing to venture out on the playground and play with us?

We would like you to try some new dating ideas. When you are dating, you are out to have some serious fun. Why not make this a game that is fun, exciting and interesting for you? If you are too serious, you can make your date feel like he/she is drowning in quick sand. The choice is yours.

If you want to get excited about meeting new people you have to be in the right frame of mind. What if we told you that each person you date will bring you closer to finding your ideal partner? Would that help you get excited? Dating is the countdown to rockets of love going off in your life. Each date gives you a piece of information to help you clarify your perfect match. You will get one of two things from meeting a new person: something you like, or something you don't like. Discovering what you don't like allows you to examine what you would like instead. If there is something you liked, it reinforces what you want and helps you stay positive on your journey to finding your ideal partner. How cool is that?

Meeting new people is the playground of self-discovery. Playgrounds can be fun unless you decide to just sit on the bench instead of getting into the game. Dating is a wonderful opportunity to discover your likes and dislikes as they pertain to relationships. In the process of having fun, you are gathering information to uncover the right relationship for you. Each new date will bring you closer to knowing the type of person that you want to spend the rest of your life with. If you learn only one thing or you confirm just one thing about what you need, want or desire, your date was a success!

First Date Fumbles

One of our favorite topics is Dating Fumbles because once you are aware of the most common mistakes, you can avoid them. Our list of dating mistakes is tried and true. If you aren't having success in dating there is a reason. If, like many of our clients, you aren't getting a second date, pay close attention to this chapter. It is hard to get a second date when you screw up on the first date. We are going to cover some of the most common mistakes made by men and women on the first date.

In coaching singles through the dating process, the biggest frustration our clients experience is not getting a second date when they really liked the person. It is a form of rejection and no one likes to be rejected.

Sometimes, you don't get a second date because the two of you just are not a good match. You don't have enough common interests to lead to a second date. Or you may lack chemistry with your date. Sometimes you just aren't attracted to the other person or they aren't attracted to you. But sometimes, even great chemistry can be killed by fatal dating errors.

Let's start at the beginning. Who asks who out? To some, we may come across as being old-fashioned. So be it. The guy should always ask the woman out. Why? Studies have shown that relationships initiated by woman usually fail. It is because men are biologically hunters. Think about it from this perspective. A man goes out hunting for a deer. When he successfully kills a deer, he is proud of his prize. That is why some men mount deer heads on their wall, as gross as that may seem to others. Now, what if we took a deer and put it in a cage and then ask the same man goes out to kill that deer. Do you think he is going to feel proud about that kill? No, because there was no challenge; there was no hunt. The same thing applies in the dating world. The man needs to feel like he has won a prize! He needs a challenge. If you take that away from him, you become like the caged deer.

Women, if you want a guy to ask you out, you have to give him some clear indication that you are interested. Smiling and eye contact go a long way in getting a man to talk to you. You can also initiate a conversation. Just don't ask him out! Let him take the lead when initiating the date or asking for your phone number.

A quick way to kill the mood on a date is to cling to a topic that is not interesting to the other person. The topic you discuss can make or break the date. On a first date, you are looking for commonality. You want to find a connection. What parts of your life are similar? You have to find something of interest to both. The more you have in common, the more success you will have not only on the date but in a potential relationship.

What if you date a guy who is rebuilding a 1968 Camaro? For the entire date, all he talks about is a chasse, fuel pump and boring this and that. He is pushing the snooze button on the date. Big snore! This is the equivalent of a woman talking about the details of a purse party she attended, describing in great detail the Prada, Burberry and Gucci knock-off purses she bought.

You should also avoid topic about politics, religion, and your ex. Talking about your ex is a big no-no. Most of what people have to say about their ex is negative. Why focus on negative things when there is so much more to discuss? Put your attention on your date. One of our clients shared a story about going on a date with a man who was a widower. During the entire date he talked about his late wife and what a wonderful woman she was. He said that it would be hard to find someone as wonderful. He did not get a second date with our client. She did not want to compete with the ghost his wife. She felt she would never measure up and quite frankly had no desire to even try. His fatal mistake was not focusing his attention on his date. He barely asked her any questions about herself.

Have a statement ready to give regarding your ex. It might be something like this. "I was married for six years. During this time I learned a lot about myself and relationships. It didn't work out because we were too young but I appreciate how much it helped me grow. I really would like to know more about you tonight." Then ASK A QUESTION! Change the subject to something more meaningful and beneficial to both of you.

One of the biggest errors people make on a first date is making the date too long. Keep it short and simple. You are just trying to get a feel for the person. If there is a match, there will be plenty of time to get to know each other.

Meet your date at restaurant or café. You can leave when you want and you won't feel pressured to invite them into your home at the end of the date. Men should meet the woman near her home. It is the gentlemen's way of dating. We don't think a man should get a second look if he expects the woman to meet him halfway. In fact, he shouldn't get the first date. Women need to be courted not only during the dating process but during the marriage, too. Men who don't court a woman will be out in the cold with anyone who is truly a good catch. Any self-respecting woman will not meet you halfway on a first date.

There seems to be a question of who should pay for the date. We strongly believe that the man should pay for the date. Men, if you can't afford to pay for the date, then chose a less expensive venue. As we said before, women need to be courted. The fact that they have a job is something men should value. It makes them a better catch. Regardless of a woman's income men, you need to whip out your wallet out faster than a hired gun in the Wild West when the bill comes. Men who expect a woman to pay will not get future dates with any worthwhile woman.

Another common mistake is revealing too much about you and your life on the first date. You want to get to know the other person, but you don't want to destroy the mystique. We all have areas in our life that aren't going well. We all have relationships that have failed and hurt us. We all have baggage. Would you dump your baggage in the lap of a stranger? We certainly hope not. Then don't do it on a first date!

We all have things from our childhood that have impacted our lives. You don't need to share these with your date until the relationship has developed more fully. You should have mutual trust before your share vulnerabilities and that develops over time. When you share too much about yourself too soon, you can scare someone off. Instead, let your date see what is wonderful about you and your life and he or she may want to become part of it. Be upbeat and positive.

Getting intoxicated will kill the mood of any first date. It should be a red flag for anyone. If someone gets intoxicated on a date they very well might have a drinking problem. More importantly, drinking lowers your inhibitions. You are likely to run your mouth about inappropriate subjects or do something you wouldn't normally do. Getting drunk is usually a surefire way of not getting to the second date. Keep drinking to a minimum. One or two drinks should be the max.

Being late for a date does not give a good first impression. Being late makes the other person feel that you had more important things to do and that their time isn't important to you. It is just plain rude.

And now, for sex! You all knew this was coming. Sex on a first date is almost always a sure way to sabotage your chance for a solid relationship. Here's why! Men, you're thinking "Cool. I get sex." Women you are thinking that you are sealing the deal now that you are sleeping together, you are in a relationship. Wrong! Wrong! Wrong! If you slept with him on the first date, how many other men have you slept with? That is not the type of woman that he brings home to meet the family or wants to be the mother of his children. He might ask you out again because he wants more sex but he usually marries someone who has enough self-respect not to "put out" early in the dating process. So what is the appropriate amount of time to wait? We recommend waiting until you are in an exclusive monogamous relationship. Once the sex starts in a relationship, the emotional development slows down tremendously. You are both looking forward to the next sexual interlude instead of getting to know each other. Getting to know each other takes a back seat to the sex.

Common Mistakes Made By Men

- Choosing a venue for a first real date is important. This usually falls on the man's shoulders. You want to make sure that you don't go too cheap. Taking her to McDonald's and telling her that she can have anything on the dollar menu is going to leave you out in the cold when you seek a second date. Going too expensive can cause a woman to feel like she has to pull out her pocketbook or that you are trying hard to impress her. Although there are many women who love being taken to a very expensive restaurant, it sets up a problem for future dates. When you choose a very expensive venue for your first date, you may have set a too high a standard for future dates. You can also cross Hooters off your choices. Their chicken wings aren't that good.

- Don't talk endlessly about sports, cars and electronics. Find a subject matter that you can both enjoy.

- Making comments about other women or flirting with other women can shut down your chance to get the second date. Your attention needs to be on her, not other women.

- A man who tells a woman repeatedly how much he likes her is heading for some serious trouble. You don't really know her that well. She likes the thrill of the chase, too. Don't kill the mystery. A man who floods a woman with too many compliments during a date can make the woman feel uncomfortable. After all, you really don't know her very well. Men who overdo the compliments seem desperate. Desperate men are not attractive.

- Don't be the "knight in shining armor." Men that try to rescue women get walked on. If your self esteem is tied up in helping someone with their job, money problem, family issues, problems with their ex etc., you are setting yourself up for a lifetime of fixing things and a very co-dependent relationship.

- Being overly chivalrous can actually backfire. Instead of showing up with a huge bouquet of flowers bring a single rose. Most women like men who open doors and pull out her chair. Unfortunately many women aren't accustomed to being treated like a lady. If you don't plan to treat her like this for the rest of the relationship, keep it to a minimum. Women complain that a man has lost interest in her when he stops doing these things.

- Don't correct her or interrupt her. Be a good listener.

- Don't let her do all the talking. You want her to get to know you as much as you want to know her.

- Don't answer your cell phone or text message someone while on a date. If you need to check on your kids, set a time to walk away from the table and call. Taking a personal or business call during a date is rude.

- Don't be rude to the waiter or service staff. Women like men who are courteous and considerate.

- Wear appropriate clothes for the date. Don't over dress or under dress. Men, plaid flannel shirts, worn-out pants or t-shirts are not impressive. Get one of your female friends to help you pick out a few great dating outfits. If you don't have any female friends, many stores have personal shoppers who can do wonders to help you look fabulous. Their service is usually free. The quickest way to ruin an entire look is wearing unpolished or dirty shoes. Invest in good pair of dress shoes that you can use for dating. Leave the basketball shoes in your closet unless you are doing something athletic on your date.

- Don't expect your date to sleep with you. It isn't even appropriate to broach the subject of sex early in the relationship. When you tease and joke around about sex, women know you are checking out your opportunity.

- Don't be wishy-washy. Women like men who can make decisions. If you can't decide what you want to order from the menu, it isn't a good sign. Don't debate for a half hour about what you are going to get. This is annoying and wastes precious time you should be using to get to know each other. When setting up the date, be confident in your choice of destination or activity. You might give them the choice between two things to do. Don't offer them a laundry list of choices.

- Don't be controlling. Taking charge of what you are both going to order is not a good idea. You don't know her taste. This is a big red flag.

    We had a client who went on a date with a self-proclaimed wine expert. When she ordered her favorite wine, he quickly voided her order with the waitress and ordered her a different wine without even asking. He did not get a second date. Don't assume that you know what she will like. This is pompous and controlling behavior.

Common Mistakes Made by Women

- Don't run your mouth off. Let your date have a chance to talk. After all, you are trying to get to know him. A huge mistake women make is dominating the conversation. They don't let the guy get a word in edgewise. They often use the rapid-fire method of communicating by jumping from one subject to the next. The guy feels like he has been trapped in a pinball machine. Then there is the woman who agrees with everything her date says. Her favorite line is, "I agree." Everything the man says makes her laugh. Men want to blow in this woman's ear just to see if they feel wind coming out the other side.

- Avoid being critical of his choice of restaurant or of the service. When you criticize his choice, you are criticizing him. Men hate women who nag and complain. Keep it to yourself. Having an attitude is not a way to impress a man.

- Don't be too flirtatious. You don't want to send the wrong message. Women, men read this as wanting sex. There is a huge difference between someone who flirts and someone who hunts. Flirting is connecting with a person and getting to know them.

Hunting is sending out the message that you are interested in a physical relationship. Keep the physical contact to a minimum. Don't keep touching him. We have to roll our eyes when a woman has been physical during the date, touching his hand, face, or thigh, but then at the end of the date when the man kisses her with some tongue action, she is offended.

- Avoid talking negative about yourself. You have way too many positive attributes to talk about without bringing up your short-comings.

- Dress appropriately. You can be cute, sexy and stylish without looking like a sex kitten. We have had several clients complain that men always want to have sex on the first date. When we evaluated dating wardrobe choices, their dating outfits consisted of short skirts, tight pants and plunging necklines. It didn't take a rocket scientist to figure out what message they were sending. Also, you don't want to show up in your favorite worn out sweat outfit either. Make a first good impression. Dress appropriately for the date. Take the time to look your best.

- The subject of marriage and your biological clock are not good subjects to bring up because this is the quickest ways to get a man to head for the hills. On an episode of The Bachelor there was a beautiful intelligent physician who talked about her biological clock. She wanted to make sure that the "bachelor" was willing to REPRODUCE in the very near future. She actually used the word "reproduce." Was she looking for love or a sperm donor? This woman was surprised, hurt and angry that she didn't receive a rose, inviting her to stay and have more dates with the "bachelor." DUH!

- Don't have sex on the first date. For that matter, hold off on sex until you are in a committed monogamous relationship. If you sleep with him on the first date, he will think that you do that with all of your first dates. That is not the impression you want him to get about you if you're hoping to get him to the altar. Once you really get to know him and have real feelings for him, the physical connection is so much more satisfying.

- Having an "attitude" will cause any self-respecting guy to delete your phone number and fast!

- Grilling him about his job, income or financial affairs sends a red flag. If you want to be viewed as a gold digger, go right ahead and ask. If his financial situation is important to you, it will be revealed in a short time. You can ask questions about his job, etc., on the third date and beyond but first you have to get the second date.

- Having a Cinderella Complex is a turn off for a balanced and confident man. Balanced men want a partner, not someone who needs rescuing.

- Some women want to impress their date with how successful they are. Being able to take care of ones self is a great quality. But don't leave your date thinking that there is no room in your life for a mate. Men need to see the softer side of a woman. Keep the talk about your career to a minimum.

If you can avoid these common dating mistakes, you have a much higher chance of landing a relationship. You might think that these are just common sense. They are! But how come so many people keep making the same mistakes over and over again?

CHAPTER 20

Great Dating Ideas

A frequently asked question seems to be, "What is a good thing to do on a first date?" The most important aspect to consider is whether the date designation gives you an opportunity to talk. Dating is the process of getting to know each other.

Do you remember back in high school and college that going to the movies was considered a good first date? The reality is that there is little talking happening in the two to three hours invested in the date. You spend most your time in silence watching the movie and eating popcorn.

First dates should be short, preferably under two hours. There is a desire to extend a date when it is going well but you always want to leave your date wanting more. When you spend too much time together, the tendency is to give your date too much information about yourself or make another first date blunder. One trick we teach our clients is to always have somewhere you need to be after the date. This forces you to keep the date short.

Here is list of our all time favorite dates:

- Bowling: It doesn't matter if you are no good at bowling. It can just be fun to laugh at your gutter balls.

- Miniature golf: It is cheaper than real golfing and a great deal of fun. You can also see how competitive your date is or whether he or she cheats.

- Sightseeing: Often we never visit the places near us and explore. Find a place that an out of town visitor might want to see.

- Comedy Club: The goal is to have fun. Finding the gift of laughter is always fun. But be prepared for raunchy humor.

- Amusement Parks: Fun, fun and more fun. There is lots of time to get to know each other while you are waiting in line.

- Wine Festival: Remember to drink in moderation on any date. Wine festivals often have live music, good food and great crafts.

- County Fair: A lot like the amusement park but with local crafts vendors and exhibits.

- Horse Races: You don't need to know anything about racing to enjoy this classic spectator sport.

- The Zoo: It is a great place to observe nature and talk.

- Get an Ice Cream Sundae: Ice cream is a timeless inexpensive treat.

- Take a Walk at Sunset: It can be romantic and it is free!

- Visit a Museum: You can take in something of interest together. This adventure is great for conversation starters.

- Share a Picnic Lunch: It is simple and no one will interrupt you by asking if you want a refill on a beverage.

- Take in Sunday Brunch: What a great way to start a day!

- Fly a Kite: Become a kid again.

- Carriage Rides: Romance at its best.

- Hot Air Balloon Rides: Take in the beauty from above. But this can be a bit pricy.

- Go Carts: As you can tell, we love bringing out the kid in you!

- Ice Skating: You don't have to be good at it to have fun!

- Jet Skiing: More fun times!

- Fishing: Great time to talk, relax and take in nature.

- Chat over a Latte or Mocha: An inexpensive date.

- Dinner out: Try new places to dine. Notice that this is last. Dates don't need to be expensive.

The dating world can be wonderful. It is an adventure. Go into it with the intent that you will have fun and learn something about yourself and your date. It doesn't need to be expensive. The number one thing is to have the opportunity to talk and connect. Some of the very best dates are absolutely free.

CHAPTER 21

Playing It Safe

The dating game has changed a great deal over the past few decades. People's options for meeting someone used to be limited by where they lived. Now there are so many ways of meeting available men and women. These days, people meet through dating services, the Internet and social clubs. Although the unlimited opportunities are exciting, it makes sense to play it safe.

Most of the things we are going to tell you in this section are common sense to most. Here is what we know about common sense. Sometimes our desire to not hurt someone's feelings gets in the way of using common sense. Both men and women have to exercise some level of common sense on a date. In the world of Internet dating and blind dating, you never know what you are walking into. The probability is that you are on a date with a really great person. However, you need to still use caution.

We have a story that might make you snap to attention and really pay heed our tips for playing it safe.

After going to the movies, two sisters went to a bar located inside of an upscale restaurant. They planned to have a couple of margaritas and go home. They easily found a table and were waiting for their server to take their order when they were approached by two, well-dressed, attractive men. They struck up a conversation and the men offered to buy them a drink. They accepted. One of the men disappeared, went to the bar and ordered the margaritas. He came back to the table with the drinks.

The man who had brought the drinks to the tables made his move on one of the sisters and convinced her to go with him to shoot some pool at a local pool hall. She agreed, but by the time she had walked to the parking lot, she realized something was wrong. She felt light-headed and physically ill.

The man had laced her margarita with heroine and GHB, the date rape drug. She had a heart condition that the drugs aggravated and she collapsed in the parking lot. When the man could not get her to his car, he left her curled up like a ball on asphalt

A Good Samaritan saw her lying in the parking lot, called 911 and she was rushed to the hospital fighting for her life.

We are not telling you this to make you fearful. We are telling you this to make you aware. Sometimes we let our guard down if we have been drinking (our inhibitions are lower when drinking) or we feel we are safe because we among people that we know. Follow a few safety suggestions to help keep you safer. There are no guarantees, but following these guidelines many help.

Tips for Having a Successful and Safe First Date

- Don't get into a car with someone that you have met in a chance meeting, this includes Internet dating. This person is a stranger. Even if the date is going well, don't get in their car.

- Take your own car to the first three to five dates or until you feel comfortable with the person. By taking your own car to the meeting place, you will eliminate that awkward moment at the door wondering you should invite the person in for coffee or a nightcap. You can leave if the date is a dud or if you feel unsafe.

- Always meet in a public place. There will be plenty of time for privacy if you want to date the person further.

- Never drink more than the equivalent of two alcoholic drinks in a two hour period of time. Alcohol impedes your judgment. Never drink a beverage that did not come directly from the bartender or waiter/waitress. Unfortunately, there are those people who put GHB (date rape drug) into drinks in hopes of getting what they want. Buy another drink instead of taking the chance.

- Limit the amount of personal information you give out. Give a cell phone number or voicemail box number, not your home number. We recommend getting a voice mailbox and an email account to use just for dating. Don't reveal where you work or where you live. Better to be safe than sorry!

- Don't say you want to see the person again if you don't. You set up expectations, hurt feeling and sometimes, those endless calls/ emails asking, "Why haven't I heard from you?" You might prevent someone from becoming a stalker.

- Always tell a friend or family member that you are going on a date and when you expect to be home. Give them all the information about the person you are meeting, where you are going and when you expect to be home. Call them if you have a change of plans while on the date. Call them when you get home. Tell them you will call them if you are planning to be late. It may sound stupid but the one time that you don't do this may be the time you wished you had. Men, you should do this too. Have you watched *Fatal Attraction*?

- Always carry a fully charged cell phone. It is just a safety precaution. You can't find a pay phone easily these days. Most cell phones have a GPS tracking system when turned on. If you are ever abducted, you may be found because of your cell phone. You can also call someone for help if needed.

- Read our list of Dating Mistakes before your date.

- Go on the date with the intent to be authentic, have fun and to always be safe.

You now have some great ideas for the first few dates. You also know how to play it safe when you go on a date. You are really ready to roll up your sleeves and address some interesting roadblocks to getting to "I do."

CHAPTER 22

Becoming an Attraction Magnet

Your ideal mate is out there and they are waiting for you. You just need attract them into your life. The process we use in our coaching practice has proven to be an ideal way of identifying and attracting the right person into your life. If you have taken the time to do the exercises in this book, you are well on your way to attracting the right person into your life.

The most important step to turning on your attraction magnet is to have a positive outlook and attitude about life in general and about the dating process. Second, you must learn to love yourself with all your imperfections and warts. Next, you need to be clear about the type of person who would be a good love match for you. Finally, you must take inspired action. That means getting out there and mingling, flirting and dating. You can meet the right person anywhere, anytime and anyplace.

We mentioned before that we made a list of the qualities that we wanted in our next relationship. We both had thought long and hard about what would make us happy. We were crystal clear that we deserved to be happy and with the right person. Then we met each other and the rest is history.

The love of your life might drop through the skylight of your home. But it is unlikely unless you are getting a new roof or there is a misdirected skydiver sailing through the sky. They might knock on your front door. But more than likely it will be a neighbor or a door-to-door sales person. You are going to have to step out into the world. But before you do, we are going to introduce you to one more amazing tool.

If you are willing to do the work, the love of your life might be one party away from becoming your soul mate. What you saw happen in our love story was the "*Laws of Attraction*" at work. We would like to introduce you to this amazing part of your world.

If you have not heard of the *Laws of Attraction*, we are pleased to be to introduce you to them. The *Laws of Attraction* impact the world around you whether you know they exist or not. The *Laws of Attraction* are called laws because they are the same for everyone.

We are all grounded to the earth by the gravity field. You can't see it, but we know it is there. At one time, we were unaware that there was gravity. It wasn't until Sir. Isaac Newton made the discovery of gravity that we began to understand it. Not knowing about gravity didn't make it any more or less real. Now that we know there is the *Law of Gravity*, we can see how it works. It is the same with the *Laws of Attraction*.

There are lots of stories floating around about the discovery of the *Laws of Attraction*. Some say that people have been aware these laws for centuries. Others believe that scientist Albert Einstein discovered these laws towards the end of his life. It doesn't really matter who discovered them. It is just nice to know they exist.

By understanding the *Laws of Attraction*, you are more likely to find your mate. For this reason, we are going to show you how to turn on your attraction magnet using the *Laws of Attraction*.

Turning on Your Attraction Magnet

There are three components to the *Laws of Attraction.*

1. *Like energy attracts like energy*

This simply means that we attract people into our life who have the same vibration of energy. If we are a positive-feeling person (not just someone who talks a good game, but who really feels good about themselves and life in general), we attract other positive people. A truly positive person can find the good or gift in any situation. If we are negative, we attract negative people. Negative people can take different forms: insecure, controlling, perfectionist, critical, worrying, or fearful. If we are coming from a place of negative vibration, we will attract someone who is also coming from a negative vibration. Birds of a feather flock together.

Remember where we started in this book? We started with YOU and where you are placing your attention. Were you listening to the Itty Bitty Shitty Committee? If so, your attention was on the negative. That is why it is important for you to pay attention to your positive attributes. If you are focused on your negative attributes, you are going to attract someone who has similar traits.

Next, we got clear about your beliefs in dating and relationships. We spent time reframing your beliefs and getting rid of the thoughts that don't serve you in a love relationship. We, then, came up with new and empowering beliefs.

Every one of these steps has helped you to turn on your attraction magnet and bring in a healthy, loving, life partner.

2. *You attract into your life whatever you give your attention, energy and focus to whether wanted or unwanted.*

You can focus your energy anywhere you desire. You can actually attract someone from your *"Don't Want"* list in your life by focusing your attention on what you don't want. By redirecting your attention and focusing on what you desire, you can attract the right partner.

This is why you made your Ideal Mate List. We asked you to refocus your attention from what you didn't want to what you do want. Not only is your list a good tool for screening potential mates, it also keeps your attention on what you desire. This is why it is so important for you to develop your Ideal Mate List and have it down on paper.

One day, we were driving our youngest daughter to cheerleading. She announced that she wanted to play a new version of the punch-buggy game. The kids use to punch each other whenever they saw a Volkswagen Bug. Instead, she wanted to punch us whenever she saw a red car. In about two minutes, we all had been punched a couple of dozen times and our arms were getting as red as the cars. Our daughter started to laugh and then said, "I didn't realize there were so many red cars on the road. I think we should stop now."

We had a new found awareness of just how many red cars are on the road because we turned our attention to the red cars. You can shift your awareness about quality singles just as easily. When you focus your attention on the positive qualities of your ideal mate, you will be surprised to see how many men/women you will find with those wonderful qualities.

3. Allowing and believing that it is truly possible to have what you desire. Allowing is the absence of doubt.

The *Law of Allowing* is a bit tougher to conquer. You might be great at deciding what you want. You can focus your energy and attention on what you desire. But can you have faith that what you desire will come into your life without having to work like a dog to get it?

In our society, we believe that you have to work hard to be successful. There is nothing wrong with that belief if you don't mind feeling like you are swimming upstream or pushing a boulder uphill. There is a much easier way.

You have probably heard from many people that they found their ideal mate when they weren't looking. There is a reason for this. These people become clear about the type of mate they wanted. Instead of being focused on the dud dates, not being asked to dance at a singles event, or brooding because it had been weeks since their last date, they relaxed. They were no longer focused on the negative.

Now, it's not productive to say, "I'm working on allowing the person of my dreams to walk into my life," and then using that as an excuse for not getting out there and meeting other single people. Part of the *Law of Allowing* is getting out there, but with the attitude that you don't have to find "the one" at each singles event. This is setting your standards way too high. Making this small, seemingly insignificant shift in your thoughts will make a huge difference. Do you remember when we mentioned the ship sailing from New York to England and how by changing course one degree it ended up in a different country? This small change in attitude is your "one degree."

If you believe you were unsuccessful when you went to a singles event because you didn't get a date or have someone ask for your phone number, you are setting yourself up for unhappiness and failure.

If you go to a singles event and you meet some nice people, the event was successful. What if you learned to salsa? Consider it a success! If you went and just had some fun, you were successful. The more you measure your success with this new "success yard stick," the faster you will meet your ideal mate.

Getting More Yardage in Your Dating Game

Why is learning about the *Laws of Attraction* important to you? The *Laws of Attraction* exist whether you acknowledge them or not. They are like the *Law of Gravity*. You don't need to know about gravity to have it impact your world and life. By knowing about the *Laws of Attraction,* you can learn to work them to your advantage.

First of all you need to understand that as a living being you are giving off a vibration every second of the day. These vibrations are either negative or positive. As we send out these vibrations, the *Laws of Attraction* are matching your vibrations and giving you more of the same.

So, where do our vibrations come from? They come from our mood or feelings. Our mood comes from our feelings.

We are going to describe a situation where the *Laws of Attraction* are at work. As you are reading this, we want you to reflect on experiences you have had in your life that might be similar. So, have you ever had an experience like this?

You stayed up late and are just plain exhausted. You do not want to get up in the morning. You finally drag yourself out of bed silently complaining to yourself about having to go to work. You start getting ready for work and you discover you are out of hair gel. Your hair looks terrible. Now you have to go to work and look crappy, too. You make toast and you burn it. Now you have to go to work without eating because you are out of time. You attempt to leave for work but the entire car is iced over. You have to defrost it before you can leave. Your late start gets you caught in traffic and you are late for an important meeting.

The vibration given off when you got out of bed was negative. It brought in more negative vibrations. The day just started to spiral into a whirlpool of negative vibrations. If a negative vibration can attract a chain reaction that looks like a train wreck, imagine what would happen if you created a positive vibration. We are going to teach you how to be more deliberate about your vibrations.

We have coached thousands of people and have noticed that most of the people we coach are not in touch with their feelings. Often people go through life not noticing how they are feeling. It is easy to get caught up in the action part of life and ignore how you are feeling unless something hits you square between the eyes and you can't ignore your feelings any longer. By becoming aware of your feelings, you can learn to shift to a positive vibration and attract more positive things and people into your life experience.

Let's explore some positive and negative vibrations. We are going to list just a few vibrations but there are hundreds of them. We have different names for different feelings, but the reality is they either feel good or they don't feel good. We are going to refer to the good feelings as positive vibrations and the bad feelings as negative vibrations. That makes it pretty simple, wouldn't you say?

Positive Vibrations	Negative Vibrations
Excitement	Anger
Gratitude	Envy
Love	Hate
Joy	Jealousy
Appreciation	Fear
Bliss	Rage

In looking at this list, can you see what might make you feel good and what might make you feel bad? Here is some play work for you. Take a piece of paper and write five more feelings that would make you feel good. Write five more feelings that make you feel bad. Now let's talk a little about how changing these feelings can shift your reality.

Shifting Your Vibration

There are many ways to shift your vibration. We are not asking you to put a happy sticker on your life. Instead, we are asking you to get connected with your feelings, thoughts, and beliefs long enough to figure out why you are not getting what you want in your life.

We live in a rush, rush, hurry, hurry world. Most of us are in such a hurry that we are constantly multi-tasking. It is not uncommon to see someone eating their lunch while driving or talking on a cell phone at the same time they are trying to pay for their groceries. It is hard to notice how you feel when you are running at warp speed.

We are typically in one of three vibrations at any given time. Once you understand where you are vibrating, you can begin to shift your vibrations to align with what you desire.

Vibration Pattern A: *The Victim*

Vibration Pattern B: *Autopilot*

Vibration Pattern C: *Positively Creating*

The Victim: This pattern shouldn't be too hard to figure out. This vibration can easily be defined by not taking personal responsibility for the things that happen in your life. People that hang out in victim mode are always blaming people and situations for their circumstances. They take limited or no responsibility for their life.

Here is the truth: We attract **every** experience into our life. Sometimes we attract what we desire. At other times, we attract what we don't want or what we fear. Whatever we are focusing on, we attract into our life.

When we learned that we controlled what we brought into our life, we had really mixed feelings. We thought, "How cool. We can control what happens in our life." On the other hand we could no longer point a finger at someone else or at a situation when life wasn't going our way. What a dilemma!

Autopilot: Have you ever driven your car to your destination and not remembered anything about the drive? Your mind has been unplugged from the world around you. You kept moving (thank goodness), but you were unaware of the journey. We often go through life on autopilot. In this rush, rush, hurry, hurry world, we are task driven. We don't plug into what is happening in the world around us. More importantly we aren't paying attention to our feelings. You are always having feelings. When you are on autopilot, you are actually in a negative vibration. You are attracting things you don't want into your experience. If you are hanging out in this vibration pattern most of the time, you aren't attracting wonderful things into your life, including your ideal mate.

Positively Creating!: Once you discover this mode, you will want to hang out there all the time. When we discovered the positively creating mode, victim and autopilot became rarely visited places. We could find a parking spot in the middle of the Christmas shopping rush. We could create money in our life easily. We started to attract positive people into our life.

Positively Creating requires that you pay attention to the world around you and to your feelings. Your feelings and moods are driving what you attract into your life.

You really have two feelings, good and bad. You can put any label on a feeling you want, but something either feels good or it feels bad. Your feelings are your inner guidance system and they were designed to be easy.

In order for you to start actively using the *Positively Creating Mode* to attract fabulous things in your life, you need to pay attention to three things.

1. You must be clear about what you desire.

2. You must stop focusing on your current situation and focus on what you want instead.

3. You have to believe that it is possible to have what you desire.

If all three of these things are in place, you will start bringing great things into your life.

So, how can you hang out in the Positively Creating Mode all the time? It is really quite simple, but it will take some retraining of your mind. The key ingredients to being in the mode of Positively Creating are appreciation and gratitude. You have to appreciate what you do have in life and be grateful for those things.

Let us give you an example: Let's say that you want to attract your ideal mate into your life but you work sixty hours a week. On the weekend, you catch up on chores around the house. Your current reality is that you are too busy to meet someone. As long as you continue to focus your attention on "I don't have enough time to meet someone," you will definitely not meet your ideal mate.

The solution is not quitting your job or letting the house go to pot. We are saying you need to switch your mindset. You can meet someone anytime and anyplace. He/She might be the man/woman behind you in the grocery store. He/She might be sitting at the table next to you at lunch or on the subway. If your belief is that you don't have time to meet someone special, you will be too busy to notice the great person standing right next to you.

Take these four steps to change your current reality to a new creative reality:

- Get clear about what you want in your ideal mate.

- Get excited about your Ideal Mate List!

- Focus on changing your reality. Instead of focusing on not having someone special in your life, notice all the great people around you.

- Believe that it is possible for you to find love. Other people are meeting their life partners every day. You will, too!

Shifting to a Winning Game Attitude

It can be hard to keep a positive attitude all the time, especially when things aren't going as you expect or desire. There are times you are going to be heartbroken on the way to finding love. It is hard to change to a positive attitude when you've been crying your eyes out all night after a break up. You have to practice shifting your attitude to a positive attitude when thing are not so volatile so when you are faced with a crisis, you can shift more easily.

Sometimes, the best way to shift your attitude and vibration is to unplug from the world and create a brief escape. So, how do you shift to a positive vibration when you realize that you are vibrating in the negative zone? We are going to walk you through a few simple ways of shifting your vibration.

Listen to Uplifting Music

Put on music that raises your mood. The music should make you want to dance and sing. Putting on uplifting music in the morning while you are getting ready for your day can really set the tone for the rest of your day. Create a play list of your favorite songs and keep it handy. A few minutes of listening to uplifting music can put the remainder of your day on the right track.

Be in the Place of Appreciation and Gratitude

A fast way to shift your energy is to identify what you appreciate or are grateful for in your life. You might have had a difficult day, but the train ran on time, and you had a great sandwich at lunch. These may be small things but take the time to focus on what is going right instead of what is going wrong.

At the end of each day, we lie in bed and recount all the things we were grateful for throughout our day. This also gives us an opportunity to show appreciation for our life and each other. We love to share those little moments during the day when we connected as a couple. It might have been that "I love you" phone call. It might have been sharing a cup of coffee in the morning. There are so many moments to be grateful for in each and every day. Whatever you pay attention to, you get more of that! So where do you want to put your attention?

Shift Your Geography

Sometimes we just need to do something different or go somewhere else to unplug from the negative vibration. A quick way of shifting energy is to take a short walk. Look around you and take in the beauty of the world.

Sometimes, we can become stuck in the mud of negative vibration. We need a longer and more compelling shift. When we really need to turn off the emotions, we like to rent one of our favorite "feel good" movies, curl up on the couch and just unplug. This allows us to reset our emotions. Then it is back to the real world, but at a higher positive vibration.

Turning Up Your Energy Meter

Refocus your energy and attention on what you want in your life instead of focusing on the things that aren't working for you. Decide what you want instead. What you "don't want" is a simply a spring board to understanding what you do want. When you are experiencing something you don't want, it allows you to ask, "If I don't want this, what do I want?" What you don't want is just the contrast to what you do want. So, contrast is not a bad thing as long as you can take the next step and identify what you desire instead. The clearer you become about what you do want, the faster it will come into your life experience.

Be careful that you aren't stating a Don't Want as a Do Want. Let us give you an example:

You just got out of a relationship that was emotionally and verbally abusive. You might say, "I want a relationship that is not abusive." By stating your desire in this way, you are still focused on the abuse. You will attract more abuse into your experience.

So, how do you refocus your attention to what you want? It might be as simple as making a one-sentence request. You might have to put down several things to get the clarity you desire. For instance, you might shift your focus to all five of the following things to get a healthy relationship free from abuse.

- I want a partner who has healthy self-esteem.

- I want a partner who loves and adores me.

- I want a partner who respects and honors me.

- I want a partner who communicates in a healthy, loving and productive manner.

- I want a partner who can take responsibility for his/her actions and behaviors.

See the difference? One is getting much clearer about what you actually desire, and the other is focusing on what you don't want. Go back to your relationship list and make sure that you have not stated any of your desires as a "don't want."

Now, you have taken major steps to shift your beliefs about yourself, dating and relationships. You have identified what you want in a life partner. Are you willing to take inspired action and go out into the dating world, have some fun and meet some interesting people? By shifting your attention and energy, you will be successful in the dating process.

CHAPTER 23

NFL (New Found Love) Game Time

If you have done all the exercises in this book, you are ready to get started on the remarkable adventure of finding your ideal mate.

You have learned to look at yourself in a different light and see the inner beauty in you. You have learned to appreciate all your wonderful qualities and see how they will play a part in finding your ideal mate. You understand what you want in your ideal mate and how to unearth your needs when dating by asking powerful questions that are respectful of another person's boundaries.

You can identify traits that might be unhealthy or undesirable in a sustainable relationship, so you can leave and find a mate who is more suited to you and your needs.

You've been given a wealth of knowledge about where to meet eligible singles and how to interact with them to increase your opportunity to date. It is time for you to make a plan to get out there and get moving! It is time to create your dating plan! This is an opportunity for you to determine how you might meet potential dates and how much time you will invest in the dating process.

Decide how much money you have to spend each month on dating or going to singles events. Are you going to spend money on Internet sites? If so, how much are you willing to invest?

How many hours per week will you spend investigating avenues of meeting singles? (Internet sites included)

How many hours per week will you devote to dating each week?

If you don't see immediate results, don't change your plan. Give it time. If you are working your plan for several months without dating, then you might consider making some changes.

Go back to the things you like to do. How can you do what you love and meet potential dates? If you do what you love, you have a higher opportunity to meet someone who has instant compatibility with you.

List five things you love and would like to do more often. Here is an example of what your list might look like.

1. Go to a wine tasting event

2. Dancing

3. Go to a karaoke night

4. Hiking

5. Reading

What are you willing to do over the next thirty days to get yourself out into the dating world? Your plan might look something like this.

Example Dating Plan

Objectives

Go on one date a week:

- Coffee

- Glass of wine

- Lunch

My Strategy

I will talk to three new people daily to increase my ability to talk to strangers and my opportunity to date.

- Attend singles events

- Join hiking club

- Take Salsa lessons

- Join an online dating site

- Go to a wine tasting event

Things to Do

- Sign up for singles group on www.meetup.com including a wine tasting group.

- Look at different Internet dating sites and see what looks good.

- Check out dancing lessons, costs, and people who attend.

- Checking out local hiking group. Ask questions about the demographics of the group. where do they hike? How often do they meet?

Timeline

- Within one week I will complete my task list.

- Within one week, I will ask someone out on a date.

- Within two weeks, I will attend a singles event.

- Within one month, I will take my first salsa lesson.

- Within one month, I will go on a hike or to an event with a hiking group.

Once you have a plan, you can get started. You can make changes as they are needed. You might need to find some single friends to go out and have fun with. Keep your eyes open. Singles events are a great way to meet new friends with common interests.

As part of your plan, review your ideal mate list weekly. Review your list of your twenty-five best qualities every single day. Put your mantras on your bathroom mirror, so you can see them often. This will help you change your inner dialog to positive dialog. You will be surprised at how quickly your life changes.

Not only will you see changes in your dating life but all your relationships will become more fulfilling and satisfying as well. Unhealthy relationships will change or fall away. You will be a new you, open to loving and being loved.

This is just the beginning of change for you. You have unlocked the secret of finding fulfilling, sustainable love. Thank you for allowing us to be part of your journey. We look forward to hearing from you when you meet your ideal mate.

EXERCISE: The Readiness Test

As dating coaches, we help single people assess their readiness for dating and being in a healthy relationship. Take the readiness test and see how ready you are to be in a committed relationship. Be objective and honest with yourself. Give yourself one point for each YES answer.

1. *I have written out a list of all the qualities I want in a life partner.*

2. *I am realistic about what I want in a partner.*

3. *I am successful in choosing men/women to date.*

4. *I have identified ten non-negotiable requirements for screening potential partners.*

5. *I have a good group of friends.*

6. *I have a successful job or career.*

7. *I enjoy spending time by myself and a partner would just be a bonus.*

8. *My life and career schedule allows quality time for a relationship.*

9. *I don't have legal ties to another relationship.*

10. *I have no unfinished emotional business with a former lover, partner or spouse.*

11. *I am happy and fulfilled by my work and can financially support myself.*

12. *I have healthy boundaries with my co-workers and boss.*

13. *My health/mental health do not interfere with a relationship.*

14. *I am reasonably happy and content.*

15. *I am actively working on my own personal development.*

16. *I pay my bills on time.*

17. *I am not overly extended with debt.*

18. *I have a healthy relationship with my ex, children, parents and siblings.*

19. *I have set healthy boundaries with family and friends.*

20. *I have chosen healthy friendships.*

21. *I don't feel the need to rescue friends and family.*

22. *I have effective dating skills.*

23. *I easily disengage love interests who are not a match to me.*

24. *I set healthy boundaries in dating and relationships.*

25. *I am not overly eager to be in a relationship.*

26. *I am committed to taking things slowly in a developing relationship and to not have sex until I have been dating more than three months.*

27. *I look for someone's words to match their actions and exit a relationship if that does not exist.*

28. *I know how to handle conflict in a relationship.*

29. *I can be intimately engaged in sharing my feelings with someone.*

30. *I am able to receive as easily as I am able to give.*

31. *I am comfortable with myself and my body.*

32. *I have healthy self-esteem.*

33. I don't have any self destructive behaviors or addictions.

34. I really believe that I am a good catch.

35. I want to be in a relationship for the right reason.

28-35 Points: *Green Light! You are ready to date. Most of your life is in order. There may be a few small tweaks to improve your dating readiness, but overall, you are raring to go.*

27-20 Points: *Yellow Light! You have some issues that still need work, but you are pretty close to being ready to enter a love relationship and be successful. Take it slow while dating and pursuing a relationship. Review the exercises in the book. If you play full out and do all the exercises, you should be ready to go soon.*

0-19 Points: *Red Light! Take a break from seeking a partner and focus on your life. If you address your issues before getting into a relationship, you will be much more successful. Sometime, seeking professional help can get you ready to date sooner. You might need some time to heal from a recent or past relationship break-up or need some specific help on boundaries or other life skill. The Cupid's Readiness Test is just a gauge to help you understand if more work is needed. The choice is yours to make.*

If you have done all the exercises in this book, you probably scored pretty well on this test. If you didn't score a green light on the test, don't get discouraged. All it that it means is that you have some work to do. Most of us do. Use the results of this Readiness Test as a compass for moving forward and successfully navigating the dating world. The test gives you an awareness of where you are right now. You can't figure out where you are going unless you know where you are.

Look and see if there is commonalty to the questions to which you answered NO. If so, there might be something specific that you should address. What is one step you can take to begin changing that situation? The process of change begins with one step. You've already taken that step by identifying that something needs to shift. Take another step and then another until you get things on track. Sometimes, the next step is hiring a professional who can guide you to success and resolution.

Remember, your life does not have to be perfect for you to enter into a relationship. If you feel good about yourself and your life, you are ready to start a relationship.

We hope this book has served as your guide to accepting yourself and claiming that you are deserving of a great relationship. Just by taking doing these two steps, you greatly increase your chances of finding great love. The type of love that fills your body, mind and spirit with a feeling of contentment like nothing you have ever felt before. It is the type of love that makes you feel desired, honored, respected and cherished for all the rest of the days you spend together. It is a love where you both grow and develop as individuals and your partner is your greatest cheerleader and supporter of your new growth and accomplishments.

We wish you happiness and a wonderful love relationship. We know that it is possible for you to have the love you deserve and desire with a soul mate connection because we have seen many people experience it and we are living proof that it exists. Love yourself and believe that it is possible for you to experience love, too. True love is on its way to you, soon!

About The Authors

Jeannine and Keith Kaiser are married and live in the San Francisco Bay Area where they have raised three children.

The Kaisers' are two of the nation's top dating coaches. This dynamic couple has been guiding singles to successfully find love since 2000. With thousands of their clients now married or in committed relationships, more and more singles are seeking the Kaisers' advice on finding healthy, passionate love.

Jeannine and Keith both attended the University of San Francisco (USF) where they earned their Bachelors Degrees in Organizational Behavior and Development. Keith went on to obtain his MBA at USF and Jeannine continued her education at the Coaches Training Institute where she earned her certificate in life coaching.

The Kaisers founded the Soul Mate Quest Mastery seminar series where they teach their secrets to sold-out crowds. The Kaisers are continuing to expand their seminar series across the United States to help more and more people find and create the love relationship they desire, but has eluded them—until now.

Soul Mate Quest Seminars

Get a 10% discount when you enroll in any of the Soul Mate Quest Mastery seminars. Just go to our website www.SMQMastery.com and enter the discount code CUPID in the promotional code line provided.

Sex and Being Single Seminar

- How to ask for an exclusive dating and sexual relationship.
- Does having sex impact the success of a relationship?
- How long should you wait before having sex?
- Why many men don't call again after having sex!
- Can you keep a man's interest without having sex?
- Why a woman's behavior changes after having sex!
- How to discuss safe sex, HIV testing and birth control.

Soul Mate Quest Seminar

- Learn the keys to finding that soul mate love.
- Raise your self-esteem and become more confident.
- Stop picking the wrong partners.
- Eliminate the blocks that are keeping love away.
- Learn the secrets to creating a soul mate relationship.
- Release the pain of past relationships.
- Design a plan to connect with your soul mate.

Dating Mastery Intensive Seminar

- Why do you keep choosing the wrong partners and how can you change these patterns?
- Learn our easy, highly-effective flirting skills.
- Double your dates by successfully working a room.
- Become a great conversationalist.

- Learn more about your dates by asking great questions.
- Write a great internet profile that will get the attention of quality singles.
- How to nicely tell someone you don't want another date.
- Learn to get the love you want.

Love Quest Mastery Intensive Seminar

- Become clear about your ideal mate and create your list.
- Eliminate your limiting beliefs about dating and relationships.
- Learn how to love in a soul mate type relationship.
- Build powerful intimacy and trust in a love relationship.
- Acquire the skills to get your needs met and meet your partner's needs.
- Create a **Dating Plan** that fits you and your lifestyle.

Decoding Men-Decoding Women Intensive Seminar

- What makes a man fall for a woman and commit?
- How you can attract a woman and have her fall for you!
- Why do men and women approach relationships differently?
- How men and women see love differently!
- Things that cause women to become needy or clingy and how to prevent this!
- What to do when a man becomes withdrawn or distant?
- Things women do that change a man from a prince into a frog!
- Things men do to turn a great woman into a shrew!
- What are the 13 Toxic Personality types to avoid in dating?
- How to know if the person you are dating is good partner material!
- What are the 50 Best Places to meet quality singles?

For more information or to register by phone:

Please call **1-888-962-8743**
or **1-888-XO-CUPID**

FREE Dating Mastery Newsletter

Register today at www.SMQMastery.com

Don't waste another minute! Sign up now for the Dating Mastery newsletter. This FREE email newsletter is designed to help single people receive dating and relationship information that will guide them to a healthy and gratifying life partner relationship. Go to www.SMQMastery.com and register today!

Delivered to your email inbox twice a month, each edition of Dating IQ has expert advice about how to maximize your dating efforts to find your ideal mate. Jeannine and Keith Kaiser, America's Dating and Relationship Coaches, keep you up-to-date by providing important information about dating and relationships. Knowledge is power. Getting the right knowledge will help you make healthy decisions and get closer to having the life you've always wanted.

And there's more! Dating Mastery newsletter subscribers get advance notice of Soul Mate Quest Mastery events and special discounts.

Help Find a Cure for Breast Cancer

Jeannine and Keith Kaiser both have been impacted by family members with breast cancer. They are committed to stomping out breast cancer in their lifetime. A portion of the proceeds of each book and seminar are donated to the Susan G. Komen Breast Cancer Foundation. Please join the Kaisers in the fight to find a cure for breast cancer.